The Mental Distillery

The Mental Distillery

Second Edition

By Ancient The Architect

To

The Student and The Teacher who becomes Master

The Mental Distillery
Copyright © 2023 by Ancient The Architect

All rights reserved. No part of this publication may be reproduced, distributed, or transmitted in any form or by any means, including photocopying, recording, or other electronic or mechanical methods, without the prior written permission of the publisher, except in the case of brief quotations embodied in critical reviews and certain other noncommercial uses permitted by copyright law.

ISBN: 979-8-218-22097-6

The information presented in this book is for general informational purposes only. The author and publisher have made every effort to ensure the accuracy and reliability of the information provided. However, they do not make any representations or warranties of any kind, express or implied, about the completeness, accuracy, reliability, suitability, or availability of the information contained in this book.

The information presented in this book is not intended to be a substitute for professional advice or guidance. Readers are advised to consult with
appropriate professionals in the specific fields related to their individual
situations and needs. The author and publisher disclaim any liability for any reliance placed on the information presented in this book.

The activities, practices, techniques, and suggestions described in this book are undertaken at the reader's own risk. The author and publisher shall not be held responsible for any direct or indirect damages or consequences arising from the use or application of the information contained in this book.

By reading this book, you acknowledge and agree to the terms of this liability disclaimer.

Cover Design: Ancient The Architect
Cover Art © 2023 Ancient The Architect
Publisher: Health Is Luxury LLC
Published in Hartford, CT USA

Introduction

In the highest spiritual context, a book of truth is not merely a collection of words but a portal to self-discovery. As you read and contemplate the teachings within, you are not simply absorbing knowledge, but rather awakening to the truth that has always been within you. The words on the pages act as a mirror, reflecting back to you the infinite potential and wisdom that resides in your true nature. Through this process, you come to know yourself in a deeper and more profound way, and in turn, you come to know the universe as a reflection of that same truth. It is a beautiful and transformative journey, one that leads to the realization that you have always known, and will always know, the ultimate truth.

The Codex

1 **What Is Mind** (1)

2 **Bulletproofing Your Mental Body** (12)

3 **SpellBreaker** (49)

4 **The Platform** (63)

5 **Live as Light** (106)

6 **Concentration** (111)

7 **ImageNation** (122)

8 **Manifestation** (142)

9 **Active Mind -vs- Passive Mind** (149)

Preface

The human mind, a vessel of infinite potential, navigates the complex seas of existence, yearning for clarity, meaning, and connection. **The Mental Distillery** is a response to that yearning—a tool designed to refine the vast and often overwhelming currents of spiritual, occult, and metaphysical frameworks into digestible, actionable insights. Much like the alchemical process of distillation, this book extracts the essence of profound ideas, transforming them into a foundation for self-knowledge, self-identity, and self-revelation.

This work is not merely a collection of theories but a guidebook for seekers, students, and teachers alike. It places the keys to spiritual growth into the hands of those who dare to ask the fundamental questions: *Who am I? What is my purpose? How can I uncover the divine within me?* Through its nine Codexes, **The Mental Distillery** invites readers to embark on a transformative journey, weaving ancient wisdom and universal truths into a cohesive map for self-discovery.

At its core, this book rests on the premise that ultimate power and knowledge lie in reconnecting with Source—the primordial essence from which all creation flows. The closer we align with Source, the more the seemingly impossible becomes accessible. Abilities we label as "psychic" or "supernatural" are revealed not as extraordinary gifts for the few but as natural byproducts of a mind and soul in harmony with the Creator's will. In this alignment, the fragmented becomes whole, and the veils between the physical and spiritual dissolve.

Each chapter, or Codex, builds upon this central idea, presenting foundational metaphysical concepts as tools for understanding the self and the universe. **The Mental Distillery** provides a roadmap to unlocking the inner cosmos. Readers are invited not only to explore the material but to embody it, becoming active participants in the process of creation.

The title ***The Mental Distillery*** was chosen with intention. Just as a distillery extracts the purest essence from raw material, this book refines the dense and often complex teachings of esoteric traditions into their most potent truths. It simplifies without diminishing, clarifies without diluting, and presents these truths in a way that honors their depth while making them accessible to all who seek them.

These chapters are not mere intellectual exercises but living practices. They invite readers to experiment with their own mind, body, and spirit, engaging with the material to bring about transformation on all levels of being. The nine Codexes are structured to illuminate the pathways to self-knowledge and spiritual mastery, providing seekers with practical tools and metaphysical insights that transcend dogma and embrace universal truths.

This book is an invitation to shift perspective, to move from passive observer to active participant, from seeker to creator. It reminds us that the power to transform ourselves and our world resides not outside us but within. The journey begins with a single question: *Are you ready to distill your mind, to uncover the essence of who you are, and to step into the fullness of your divine potential?*

The time to seek is now.
The time to know is now.
The time to become is now.

First Codex

What is mind?

The mind is a mystical and creative faculty of the soul, a divine tool that enables us to perceive, create, and connect with the spiritual realm. It serves as a mirror of the self, reflecting the soul's essence and facilitating interaction within the mental universe. Acting as a bridge between the mundane and the celestial, the mind beholds the image of God and becomes the throne upon which the soul sits.

Within the mind, thoughts are generated and consciousness is downloaded. It is the prism through which the soul projects its light onto the physical plane, illuminating the path toward enlightenment. The mind is the matrix of the mental universe—a sacred space where one engages with creation and receives divine downloads. As you navigate life, your energy field becomes tangible through the intricate workings of the mind, translating spiritual essence into lived experience.

In this sacred domain, consciousness takes form, manifesting thoughts and realities. From the crown of your head to the soles of your feet, the mind operates as a quantum instrument of the higher self, entangling with all things across worlds and dimensions. It serves as a receiver of divine light, channeling the wisdom of the higher self. Yet, it is vital to distinguish the mind from the brain, which is merely an organ of the physical body.

The higher self, the "witness", ever watchful, observes the mind's experiences and uses it as a vehicle for spiritual growth and exploration. The higher self is a fractal of the divine, a reflection of God's infinite wisdom and grace. Through the mind, it guides us toward deeper understanding and alignment with the Source.

The mind is a form of matter—though invisible to the human eye, it exists as a subtle, intangible substance that can be touched through consciousness. When you teach, for instance, you are touching the mind, transmitting vibrations that manifest as emotions, thoughts, information, and awareness. These vibrational energies travel through the ethers, which serve as the medium for the transmission of all forms of energy.

We exist in a creation composed entirely of vibrations—waves of energy oscillating at various degrees, permeating the ethers. In this mental universe, all things respond to thought, the creative product of the mind. Thoughts are particles of potential, energetic seeds wrapped in what are known as elementals. These elementals are invisible entities that move through the ethers, gravitating toward energy fields or thought forms. They clothe these thoughts, aligning with their complementary vibratory frequencies, and accumulate to manifest perceivable forms.

The mind's fabric is interwoven with elementals, which shape the energy field around you, creating forms and structures from thought. Messages can travel through this energy field, carried by unseen entities that act as messengers. These messengers move toward their intended recipient, releasing a specific energy or message into the receiver's consciousness.

When the recipient perceives this transmission, it generates a thought, idea, or feeling—for example, a mother mentally sending the message "come home" to her son. In earlier times, before the advent of modern technology, this form of mental communication was more common. A mother could send out a thought, and her child would receive it as an intuitive feeling of needing to return home. While modern technologies like cell phones and the internet have altered these natural transmissions, the underlying mechanism of thought-to-thought communication remains a profound truth of our interconnected mental universe.

The ego is the distorted reflection of the mind on the physical plane, a shadow of the true self. It emerges from the mind's attachment to the material world and its identification with the body. The ego perpetuates the illusion of separation, individuality, and limited existence. When the ego dominates, mistaking itself for the true self, it creates a false sense of isolation from the rest of creation, leading to suffering and delusion.

In contrast, the higher self is the true image—a divine spark that exists beyond the boundaries of time and space. Only by recognizing the higher self as the true source of being can one transcend the ego's limitations and awaken to their authentic nature. The mind, serving as a tool of the higher self, enables interaction with the mental universe and the manifestation of desires into physical reality. However, this same mind can also act as a barrier, veiling the true self and obscuring the inherent unity of all existence. Positioned as the interface between the physical and spiritual realms, the mind has the dual potential to either illuminate or obscure our perception of truth.

The veil that shrouds the inner light is woven from thoughts, memories, and beliefs accumulated over lifetimes. Each lifetime adds a new layer to this veil, either thickening the obscurity or allowing greater glimpses of the truth. These layers of the veil correspond to different levels of consciousness, shaped by past experiences and belief systems. The veil reflects and projects one's current state of awareness, mirroring the soul's journey and lessons.

As the soul progresses, it sheds old veils and weaves new ones, each tailored to the lessons and experiences needed for that particular lifetime. The fabric of these veils may differ—some lifetimes presenting more intricate patterns and complexities than others—but their purpose remains constant: to provide a framework for the soul's growth and evolution. When consciousness expands, lifting the veil, the soul glimpses beyond the limitations of its current experience, accessing the higher wisdom and guidance of the divine. This is the state of enlightenment, where the individual perceives the eternal truth beyond the veil of illusion created by the mind and ego.

The process of lifting the veil involves dissolving the strands of thought that weave the fabric of illusion and darkness. This allows us to move beyond the limited perspective of the ego and experience direct awareness of reality. When the veil is lifted, we come into contact with the light of the higher self. The mind is no longer a restrictive box confining our experiences but becomes a powerful tool, enabling us to embrace our true nature as fractals of God.

As a society, we are profoundly influenced and shaped by collective ideas and beliefs. Even our social and economic structures are products of the thoughts and perceptions of others. Our perception of reality is shaped by how the mind reacts to stimuli, and all our interactions with the world are filtered through this mental lens. In this reality, the mind is the operating framework for our entire being. It radiates as an energy field, encompassing us from the crown of our head to the soles of our feet, forming the center of our existence.

All entities within creation navigate reality through the mind. The body, with all its intricate systems, functions merely as an extension of the mind. Everything we experience is a manifestation of mental activity. When we gaze into a mirror, the reflection we see is not merely a physical likeness but an external representation of an aspect of the mind. Our bodies are extensions of the mind, and our sense organs act as tools, gathering information from the matrix of reality to guide the mind in navigating existence.

Indeed, all is mind, and the universe itself is fundamentally mental. But what does it mean to say the universe is mental? To explore this, consider the concept of creation. To create something, one typically needs ingredients. Yet, in a hypothetical scenario where no ingredients exist, how could anything come into being? The only way is through the power of the mind. Just as when you conceive an idea, you may initially lack physical materials, but the idea still exists vividly in your mind's eye.

For the Creator, the act of thinking brings things into existence instantaneously, while we, as human beings, manifest things at a slower pace. The Creator's process is beyond human comprehension but exemplifies the immense power of the mind. We, too, manifest through our thoughts, albeit to varying degrees. The clearer and more vivid our imagination, the more efficient the process of manifestation becomes, allowing us to align closer with the creative power of the divine.

Those who hold dominion over the world do so by manipulating your thoughts and mental imagery. Through subtle and insidious methods—cartoons, movies, music, news propaganda, and even the educational system—they gradually program your mind, often without your conscious awareness. Society operates as a vast network of mental manipulation, a matrix designed to guide and restrict your participation within its boundaries. Look around, and you will notice that your choices are often predetermined: attending schools, purchasing goods and services in a prescribed manner, and adhering to specific financial values. This creates a financial matrix that ensnares countless individuals, most of whom remain unaware of the pervasive influence of external forces. Few are taught to think critically or independently. Many rely on the thought patterns of others rather than exercising their own minds. A true critical thinker—someone who claims autonomy over their mental processes—would inevitably resist the confines of this mental matrix.

We have been conditioned to accept poverty as a natural state, but this belief is a distortion. True prosperity aligns with the essence of creation. Do not be deceived into thinking that a spiritual journey necessitates living in lack; poverty itself is an illusion.

True spiritual abundance encompasses material, mental, and spiritual prosperity. It is holistic, excluding nothing and embracing all aspects of existence.

The goal is to access and harness power while we are in these physical bodies—here and now. We are on a path of continual refinement, progressing toward perfection. Beings on higher planes of existence do not face the afflictions of sickness, poverty, or the limitations that we encounter on the physical plane. Their experiences transcend these earthly struggles, elevated by their alignment with higher truths.

As inhabitants of this plane, we pursue power to address the challenges that plague us—poverty, illness, ignorance, and even death. Every illness can be cured; the only reason such conditions persist is because of our limiting beliefs. Our thoughts shape our reality. If we believe something is incurable, it becomes so. Recognizing the immense power within us is essential, for we have been wielding it all along, often without conscious awareness.

When we face unfavorable conditions, it is often because we have directed our mental power ineffectively. Negative thought patterns, compounded by detrimental habits, hinder our ability to achieve. As spiritual beings inhabiting this physical plane, our purpose is to develop the ability to think correctly, guided by accurate knowledge.

In "reality," time does not exist—clocks do. Yet, on this plane, time appears to govern our experience. This illusion of time provides a framework for perceiving the relationship between cause and effect.

Time separates events, granting us—beings at a slower vibratory frequency—the ability to observe and understand the unfolding of reality according to our level of development. Reality itself vibrates at a rate beyond our current perception, awaiting our alignment with higher awareness.

Thought Form

The world and your reality are filtered through the lens of your accumulated thought forms, much like how eyeglasses bend light to shape your vision and perception. The words you choose to label these thoughts further influence your understanding, but it's vital to remember that the universe does not operate in English—or any human language. Language is a construct of the human mind, and while it can be a tool for expression, it also has the potential to distort perception. Words shape our understanding of reality, but linguistic patterns and cultural influences often impose biases that obscure the truth. By becoming mindful of the language we use and the meanings we assign to words, we can better align our thoughts with clarity and purpose. True connection with the universe lies not in lengthy conversations, but in cultivating awareness of its essence—and your role within it.

As a conscious being, you are fundamentally a product of the mind—a mental creature shaped by thought and intention. The very essence of the Universe is rooted in the mental realm, and your interaction with the external world primarily unfolds on this plane. Through the faculties of your mind, your body responds, aligning itself with your thoughts and intentions.

The thought forms you generate, combined with the vibrational frequencies of the words you articulate, initiate intricate chemical reactions within your being. These reactions shape the biochemical network that underpins your physical existence. Your thoughts and intentions, in harmony with your mental processes, actively influence the composition and arrangement of these chemical structures, molding the fabric of your biological and psychological reality. In this dynamic interplay, your mind becomes the architect of your experience. The world, in turn, functions as a vast laboratory, where conscious beings—much like chemical elements—interact, transforming and influencing the collective whole.

Each thought we generate weaves a unique thread into the fabric of the universe. Like a skilled director, the universe orchestrates these thought forms, shaping the experiences and interactions that define our lives. Thoughts also wield profound influence over the physical body, triggering chemical reactions and creating molecular structures that affect our overall well-being. They resonate deeply within us, shaping the vibrational frequencies of both body and mind. By cultivating intentional and harmonious thought forms, we can unlock the potential to achieve perfect physical and mental health through the interplay of chemistry and vibration. Mastering the power of thought, alongside our emotions and senses, empowers us to manifest optimal health and transform our reality. Through this awareness, we become conscious creators, actively shaping our lives and realizing our deepest aspirations. Yet, with this power comes great responsibility. The choices we make determine whether we align with the forces of light or darkness, governed by the immutable law of compensation.

Thought forms are the foundational building blocks of the universe, shaping both perception and experience. The expansion of consciousness is a journey of broadening awareness, enabling us to perceive truth without the distortions or filters of lower thought. As the higher faculties of the mind awaken, we gain direct insight into the nature of reality. Everything in existence begins as a wave of vibration, remaining formless until it interacts with a conscious mind. This interaction, perhaps governed by a fractal code, causes the wave to collapse into a specific form. To access phenomena in higher dimensions, the mind must undergo a process of purification—freeing itself from scattered, random thoughts and attaining a state of clarity. In this state, the mind becomes a mirror, reflecting the radiant illumination of the higher self onto the realms beyond ordinary perception. This illumination resonates across space and time, bridging higher dimensions and collapsing their infinite possibilities into observable manifestations, accessible to the conscious observer.

All of creation is the manifestation of the divine thought form of "God." We exist and have our being within the infinite mind of God, who continually holds us—and all that exists—in thought. Hypothetically, if God were to stop thinking, all of creation would dissolve into nothingness. The Creator is ultimately a frequency, incomprehensible to the human mind and imperceptible to our current field of awareness in its purest form. At the heart of infinity, God's presence is omnipresent, permeating every aspect of existence, while its boundaries remain undefinable and elusive.

To explore the nature of God, we can begin by meditating on the concept of "pure" consciousness. When we contemplate pure consciousness, we align our energy with the Source, harmonizing with the Creator. This practice allows us to become attuned to the highly vibrational energies that surround us—energies often misunderstood or unnoticed due to the limitations of our awareness. God is continuously emanating an unimaginable power, which at its extreme polarity becomes geometricized into the structures of creation. By reverse engineering this process, we can direct our contemplation toward pure consciousness and uncover deeper truths.

Pure consciousness transcends sound, color, thought, sensation, or any focus on chakras or abstract concepts. It is the essence of being itself, a profound awareness that underlies all existence. There is only one Source of consciousness, present everywhere at once. By immersing ourselves in this awareness, we harmonize with the Creator and open ourselves to profound revelations.

It is important to recognize that pure consciousness cannot be fully grasped by the limited scope of human understanding. However, through dedicated meditation and contemplation, we can cultivate a deeper connection to this divine energy, expanding our awareness and aligning with the higher vibrational frequencies of the universe. This journey leads to spiritual and mental growth, unlocking profound insights that guide us toward greater harmony with the Source and our higher selves.

Second Codex

Bulletproofing your mental body

Harnessing the power of your will is essential for aligning your mind with specific energetic fields. Willpower is more than mere determination—it is the active expression of your ability to focus and direct energy. However, to wield this power effectively, your will must be guided by truth, knowledge, and understanding. Willpower, when left unguided, can scatter energy or manifest outcomes misaligned with your higher purpose. When harmonized with divine will, your personal will transcends the ego's desires and aligns with the greater universal flow. This alignment allows your actions to become direct manifestations of divine intention. As you cultivate your intuitive faculties, you will increasingly recognize the subtle guidance of this higher will, enabling your thoughts and deeds to radiate a distinctly divine vibration that shapes your reality on the physical plane.

When you consistently radiate love from your heart, you not only transform your own energetic state but also influence the energy fields of those you encounter. Love is not merely an emotion but a universal vibration that harmonizes and elevates. By consciously embodying this frequency, you become a beacon of light, awakening love in others and dissolving discordant energies in your environment. Conversely, harboring ill will or resentment sends disruptive vibrations into the mental space of others, perpetuating cycles of negativity.

Advanced beings, through years of inner work, develop the ability to emanate high-level vibrations that raise the vibratory rates of everything within their sphere of influence. You, too, can become such a catalyst, promoting growth, harmony, and vitality even in the most desolate situations.

To achieve this, you must practice intentionality, consciously aligning your will with the energetic state you wish to embody. Intention acts as the foundation upon which your reality is built. Guard your mental space vigilantly, refusing to allow the projections of fear, hatred, or lack from others to infiltrate your consciousness. This includes being mindful of external influences, such as fear-based news programming or conversations rooted in ignorance and negativity. The wisdom of "as you think in your heart, so you are" underscores this truth. Here, the heart represents the center of your being, encompassing the seven major energy centers or chakras. Each chakra vibrates at a unique frequency, and when your thoughts harmonize with these frequencies, you activate their potential to influence your actions and transform your reality. By cultivating independent, conscious thought and holding steadfastly to the reality you desire, you demonstrate your readiness to receive and manifest it.

Emotions are another key aspect of this dynamic. If you find yourself overwhelmed by intense or negative emotions, redirect your focus immediately. Instead of fixating on the external trigger, mentally detach from it and observe the emotion as a separate entity. By remaining neutral and unattached, you allow the pendulum-like swing of emotions to stabilize naturally.

This practice, rooted in mindfulness and detachment, helps you connect with the spiritual energy within, disentangling from emotional turbulence and restoring inner balance. In doing so, you reclaim your power and align your mental and emotional states with higher vibrational frequencies, enabling you to move forward with clarity and purpose.

Intuitive Positioning

Intuition is the innate faculty through which we access knowledge that transcends ordinary perception. It connects us to the cosmic mind, the boundless reservoir of universal wisdom that underlies all existence. Developing this ability is essential for navigating the unknown, uncovering profound insights, and aligning ourselves with the deeper truths of reality. Intuition bridges the gap between the conscious mind and higher realms of knowledge, acting as a subtle yet powerful guide on our spiritual journey.

To cultivate intuition, we must first cultivate a receptive and clear state of mind. This requires quieting the mental chatter—the "static" of random thoughts that obstruct the intuitive flow. Approach the mental universe with curiosity and intention, consciously tuning your awareness to specific frequencies or fields of knowledge. Just as a radio must be precisely tuned to pick up a clear signal, your mind must align its energy with the vibration of the insights you seek. Release distractions, focus your senses, and allow the answers to emerge naturally into your field of awareness.

Intuitive knowledge often reveals itself in moments of silence, making it vital to learn the art of quieting the mind and creating a space for clarity.

Practicing meditation on concepts such as wisdom, intelligence, and truth can amplify this receptivity. Through meditation, you attune your consciousness to higher frequencies, inviting flashes of understanding to arise within you. These "flashes" are raw packets of intelligence—rapid vibrations carrying intuitive insights. At first, they may appear fleeting, but with practice, you can learn to slow them down, observe them clearly, and comprehend their depth and meaning. Cosmic intelligence is always present, flowing ceaselessly around and within us. However, the constraints of a restless or preoccupied mind often prevent us from registering this higher knowledge. By releasing these mental limitations, you unlock the immense potential of your intuition.

Building concentration and observation skills forms the foundation for developing intuition and expanding understanding in all areas of life. Concentration anchors your awareness, while observation hones your ability to discern the subtleties of what is being revealed. When seeking knowledge, approach the process with a silent and focused mind. Pose your questions deliberately, allowing the stillness to guide you. If the answers do not immediately surface, repeat your inquiry with patience and openness. In this space of quiet receptivity, flashes of insight will emerge—sometimes in the form of images, feelings, words or sounds. These intuitive responses are the voice of the cosmic mind, providing guidance and clarity.

As you embrace this practice, you refine your ability to capture and interpret these flashes of intuitive wisdom, enabling them to guide you toward deeper self-discovery and understanding. Each moment of intuitive alignment strengthens your connection to the universal intelligence and empowers you to navigate life's complexities with grace and purpose. The more you trust and engage with this faculty, the more seamlessly intuition will become an integral part of your daily experience, illuminating your path and revealing profound truths about yourself and the universe.

Psychic Energy

Psychic energy refers to the subtle, ethereal energy that flows within and around us. It is the energy that allows us to connect with and access information from the universal storehouse of knowledge. To tap into this higher vibrational energy and receive downloads of information, it is essential to align your mental frequency with the desired frequency, much like tuning into a specific radio station. Psychic energy, while abundant, requires intention and discipline to access and cultivate.

To increase psychic energy, several factors come into play. First and foremost, it is crucial to protect yourself from energy siphoners—people, situations, or even thoughts that drain your vitality. These energy siphoners, often referred to as "energy vampires," can deplete your energy field without you even realizing it. Surround yourself with positive, supportive people, and establish energetic boundaries to maintain and preserve your strength. Protecting your energy is not selfish—it is necessary.

Additionally, proper eating habits play a significant role. The food you consume directly impacts your physical and energetic well-being. A diet rich in high-vibrational foods, like fresh fruits, vegetables, and natural whole foods, supports the alignment of your body and spirit with higher frequencies.

Developing proper thought forms is another vital aspect of increasing psychic energy. Your thoughts shape your reality. By cultivating positive, empowering thoughts and practicing mindfulness, you create an energetic environment conducive to higher vibrations. This includes using affirmations, focusing on constructive ideas, and replacing negativity with uplifted mental patterns. Remember, your mind is the center of your energy, and whatever resides there will ripple outward into your life.

However, it is important to understand that psychic energy has polarity. It ranges from highly vibrational at one end to lower frequency at the other. Energy naturally flows from higher to lower frequencies. When we attract more energy to ourselves, it often fills the lower aspects of our being first. For this reason, purification is essential. If your mind, body, and heart are not purified, the energy you attract could amplify unresolved fears, negative thoughts, or base instincts instead of higher aspirations. This is why the process of increasing psychic energy isn't just about generating more—it's about refining and elevating your consciousness to ensure the energy aligns with your highest intentions.

In the realm of energy, neutrality is key. Psychic energy is neither inherently good nor bad—it simply exists, pure and unfiltered. Its effect on your life depends entirely on how you choose to use it. This energy has the potential to amplify and elevate your existence or, if mishandled, to dismantle and destabilize it. Energy doesn't conform to the confines of right or wrong; instead, it aligns with the direction of your consciousness and intentions. It's a powerful force meant to be harnessed for higher purposes, guiding you on your perpetual journey toward self-mastery and perfection.

However, this energy demands respect and care. Without proper preparation, its intensity can overwhelm, and those who misuse it may find themselves consumed by its allure, transforming into malevolent beings. This underscores the importance of approaching energy work with integrity and clarity. Purifying the triad of mind, body, and heart is not just beneficial—it is essential. By doing so, you ensure that the energy you cultivate aligns with your higher nature, empowering you to create harmony and contribute to the greater good.

To shield oneself from the parasitic grasp of energy siphoners, it is crucial to master the art of erecting mental barriers. These siphoners, whether people, situations, or even subtle energetic forces, can drain your vitality if left unchecked. Building strong defenses within and around oneself is not just a practical skill—it is a spiritual imperative. By polarizing your mind toward a clear and purposeful goal, you can defend your energy as if engaged in an epic cosmic battle, where every thought and intention acts as a soldier in your defense.

It is essential to minimize the tendency to engage with every fleeting sensation. Refrain from being ensnared by the constant stimuli of the physical world—every sound, scent, or passing gust of wind. These distractions, though seemingly harmless, can fragment your attention and drain your energy. Instead, cultivate an unwavering resolve to remain centered, redirecting your focus toward higher realms of consciousness. This disciplined approach preserves your vitality and ensures your energy flows toward elevated states of awareness and spiritual growth.

Moreover, maintaining a constant state of readiness is key. This readiness isn't about tension but rather about an alert presence—a state of being fully attuned to the flow of life. In this state, you are better equipped to recognize and seize the moments of opportunity that arise along your path of spiritual ascent. These moments, like windows into higher dimensions, are subtle and fleeting, but with the right mental posture, you can step through them with purpose and clarity.

The responsible and conscious use of energy is paramount, both for personal evolution and for contributing to the collective upliftment of humanity. Energy, when purified and directed with intention, becomes a powerful tool for the development of your higher nature. Guarding against egoistic tendencies and lower impulses is essential to ensure that the energy flows toward positive and transformative purposes. Redirecting potent forces, like sexual energy, to higher spiritual centers strengthens your connection to higher frequencies and aligns your actions with your divine purpose.

Ultimately, a purified and disciplined mind acts as a bulwark against the potential misuse of psychic energy. It ensures that the energy you cultivate does not feed base instincts, ego-driven desires, or harmful tendencies. Instead, it channels energy toward wisdom, compassion, and spiritual enlightenment. Energy, in its essence, is impartial—it simply follows the laws that govern its flow. Its virtue or malevolence lies entirely in the hands of the wielder. This is why embodying goodness, integrity, and higher intentions is not just wise—it is necessary. Humanity's destiny hinges on how we choose to direct the energy within us, making it imperative to align with principles that uplift and transform.

Repairing the Auric Field

The auric field, often referred to as the energy body or subtle body, is a dynamic field of energy that surrounds and protects you. It reflects your emotional, mental, and spiritual state, serving as both a shield and a mirror of your inner being. Just as trees and plants possess an auric field, so do we—and our auric fields resonate naturally with the energy of the natural world. This resonance makes nature a powerful ally in the process of repairing and strengthening the auric field.

Spending time in a garden, surrounded by the vibrant energy of plants and flowers, can help cleanse and rejuvenate your auric field. Plants emanate a gentle, harmonious vibration that interacts with your energy body, soothing disturbances and filling voids with vitality. Meditating in a forest amplifies this effect. Forests are reservoirs of life force, where the combined energies of trees create a unified frequency that deeply nourishes the auric field. Simply sitting under a tree, resting your back against its trunk, and maintaining physical contact allows you to tap into its steady and grounding energy. Trees, especially large and ancient ones, act as conduits between the Earth and the heavens, offering stability and spiritual nourishment to those who seek their support.

Another powerful technique for repairing the auric field involves a meditative connection with the Sun. The Sun, as the source of life and creative energy on this plane, radiates pure and unbounded light that can cleanse, empower, and realign your auric field. Begin by directing your mental focus toward the Sun. Envision yourself stepping into its radiant energetic space, as if you are bathing in its golden light. Imagine the warmth and brilliance of the Sun enveloping your entire being, penetrating every layer of your auric field, and dissolving any distortions or blockages. Allow its creative energy to weave through your energy body, filling it with strength and vitality.

Spend several minutes in this state, fully immersed in the Sun's light and energy. Visualize your auric field expanding, becoming vibrant and radiant, as it harmonizes with the pure frequencies of the Sun. When you are ready, gently return your focus to your physical body, bringing with you the empowerment and renewal gained during the meditation. This practice not only repairs but also fortifies your auric field, creating a protective and resilient energy body that enhances your psychic energy and overall well-being.

The key to repairing and maintaining a strong auric field is consistency. Make time to immerse yourself in the energies of nature and engage in practices that align you with universal forces. Whether through the nurturing embrace of trees, the quiet hum of a garden, or the powerful radiance of the Sun, these interactions help you cultivate a balanced and resilient energy body. Your auric field is a reflection of your connection to the greater whole, and by nurturing it, you not only strengthen yourself but also deepen your alignment with the universe itself.

Clothes and Energy

The clothes we choose to wear are more than mere coverings for the body; they can profoundly influence our energy field. This is because every fabric carries its own vibrational frequency, and these frequencies interact with our auric field, either supporting its natural flow or disrupting it. Clothing becomes an extension of our energy body, so the materials we wear can either amplify or diminish the harmony of our vibrations.

Take polyester, for example. As a synthetic material, it is widely used in modern clothing due to its affordability and durability. However, polyester often acts as a constricting force on the auric field, creating a barrier that limits its expansion and restricting the natural flow of energy. When worn, it can cause subtle energetic stagnation, leaving you feeling less vibrant and connected.

In contrast, natural fabrics such as pure silk, linen, and organic cotton resonate more harmoniously with our energy field. Silk, with its smooth and delicate texture, has long been revered for its ability to amplify the auric field, enhancing the flow of subtle energy throughout the body. Linen, derived from the flax plant, is another powerful ally for the energy body. Its natural fibers vibrate at frequencies that align beautifully with the human energy field, promoting balance, flow, and expansion. These fabrics support the auric field's ability to interact freely with the surrounding energy, cultivating a greater sense of alignment and vitality.

Color, too, plays a significant role in how clothing affects our energy. Each color vibrates at a unique frequency, influencing both our emotional and mental states. Red, for example, is associated with passion, vitality, and grounding energy, making it a powerful choice for those seeking to energize their root chakra or boost physical strength. Blue, on the other hand, emanates a calming and tranquil energy, helping to soothe the mind and promote clarity. Colors like green align with growth and healing, while white embodies purity and spiritual elevation.

When selecting your clothing, it is wise to be mindful of both the fabric and the color. By choosing natural materials that allow your energy to flow freely and selecting colors that align with your intentions, you can actively enhance your well-being. For instance, wearing linen in calming shades like pale blue or white can create a harmonious energy field, while wearing silk in vibrant hues like red or orange can amplify confidence and vitality. These choices not only impact your personal energy but also influence how you connect to the world around you.

Clothing, though often overlooked, is a powerful tool for cultivating energetic balance. Every choice you make—from the fabric to the color—can either support or inhibit your energy flow. By consciously selecting clothing that aligns with your natural vibrations, you create an environment where your auric field can thrive, expanding your connection to the universe and enriching your sense of harmony and well-being.

Responsible Attitude

It is essential to recognize that our thoughts and emotions are powerful vibrations of energy that shape our reality and influence our overall well-being. While it is tempting to blame others for the negative emotions we feel or the pain we experience, the truth is that these emotions are generated within us by our own thoughts and reactions. No one can truly "make" us feel anything without our mental consent. This is why cultivating mental fortitude and emotional resilience is so critical. If someone can hurt your feelings or cause you to react negatively, it signals a gap in your mental defenses—a lack of fortitude that must be addressed. To protect yourself fully, you must "bulletproof" your mind. Once your mind becomes impenetrable, negativity will have no foothold in your consciousness, and no external force will be able to disrupt your peace.

A responsible attitude toward energy also means learning how to engage with others wisely. One way to maintain a positive energetic state is to have a warm and open heart toward happy people, allowing their joy to resonate with your own. At the same time, it is equally important to develop understanding, compassion, and mercy for those who are struggling or unhappy. These individuals often need a kind and supportive presence to help elevate their energy. However, you must also be discerning. Some people carry deeply negative or even malicious energy that can harm your auric field if allowed to infiltrate. In such cases, it is crucial to mentally, physically, and energetically avoid their influence. This may require distancing yourself from certain individuals or environments that are not conducive to your well-being, no matter how difficult it may feel to do so.

Protecting your energy field also requires mindfulness in your reactions to negativity. Anger, in particular, can be a destructive force that clouds your judgment and disrupts the natural flow of your thoughts. When you give in to anger, your mind temporarily loses its ability to function properly, leaving entry points for negative energy to seep into your auric field. This is why it is essential to remain vigilant and not allow yourself to become reactive in the face of provocation. Understand this: your enemy may deliberately seek to anger you as a way to disarm your thinking and compromise your inner balance. Be wary of this tactic, and never allow anger to rob you of your power.

Cultivating inner peace is the cornerstone of mental and emotional resilience. Even in the presence of difficult people or challenging situations, a calm and centered attitude can act as your shield. By maintaining a state of peace, you close the door to negative energy and strengthen your ability to navigate life's trials with clarity and grace. Peace does not mean passivity—it is an active state of control over your mind and emotions, a conscious decision to protect your energy field from harm.

Ultimately, taking responsibility for your thoughts, emotions, and reactions empowers you to master your energy field. Through discipline, compassion, and unwavering self-awareness, you can create an unshakable foundation that allows you to thrive, no matter what external forces may arise.

Watch Your Tone

Every aspect of your being—from your physical body to your cells, down to the tiniest particles—vibrates at specific frequencies. Your health, well-being, and even your consciousness are directly linked to the harmony of these vibrations. You are like a living symphony, where each part of you contributes to a grand, unified melody. When your vibrations are harmonious, you radiate health and vitality. In essence, health and vibration are synonymous with music, as everything in existence carries its unique resonance, forming a universal symphony. Your personal resonance reflects your state of being and serves as your energy signature, detectable in both the physical and spiritual planes.

When you consume unnatural foods, you introduce dissonance into this symphony. Each food carries its own vibration, its own "song," which integrates into your body's melody. Unnatural or processed foods carry chaotic vibrations that disrupt the natural harmonics of your being. This disharmony damages your energy field, causing your aura to contract and draw closer to your body as a protective mechanism. Over time, this disruption can lead to imbalances in your physical, mental, and spiritual states, reducing your vitality and your ability to align with higher frequencies.

Just as food affects your vibrations, the music you listen to also impacts your energetic and physical health. Chaotic tones, such as dissonant or harsh music, can overwhelm your senses and disturb your inner harmony. This disruption triggers a stress response in your body, leading to heightened anxiety, discomfort, and even physical strain. Elevated heart rate, increased blood pressure, and weakened immune function are just some of the consequences of exposing yourself to these dissonant frequencies.

In contrast, music with harmonious tones—such as jazz or classical compositions—can elevate your mental and physical states. Jazz, with its intricate improvisations, challenges the brain's cognitive abilities, activating areas responsible for attention, memory, and pattern recognition. This heightened demand stimulates neural pathways, encouraging mental agility and creative thinking. Classical music, with its structured and complex nature, engages the brain's spatial-temporal reasoning skills. The interplay of melodies, harmonies, and dynamics in classical compositions encourages problem-solving, organizational thinking, and the ability to perceive relationships between objects and ideas. This is more than entertainment—it is a profound interaction between sound and consciousness, capable of aligning your inner symphony with the greater harmonics of the universe.

When your body and mind vibrate in harmony, you align with the right tone of the universe. This alignment allows you to expand—not only energetically, as your aura extends and radiates outward, but also in your consciousness. Self-awareness deepens, and your knowledge of self grows. This expansion mirrors the continuous growth of the universe itself, an eternal dance of vibration and creation.

The more you attune to harmonious vibrations, the more you embody the universal symphony, becoming a reflection of its beauty and balance.

To maintain this alignment, be mindful of what you consume—whether it is food, music, or even thoughts. Each choice contributes to the vibrational field you create. When you choose harmony, you invite expansion, clarity, and alignment with the divine frequencies that govern the cosmos.

Sound

Sound is a profound force that directly impacts our energetic state. It is a powerful vibrational medium capable of either enhancing or disrupting our energy field. Everything in existence vibrates, and sound waves, as carriers of these vibrations, travel through the ethers, interacting with us on physical, mental, and spiritual levels. The sacred sound of "Om," for instance, is not merely a vibration but a spiritual anointing, signifying the awakening and alignment of the spiritual aspirant. When experienced in meditation, the sound of "Om" resonates through the layers of our being, harmonizing and connecting us to the divine source.

Sound vibrations, whether harmonious or discordant, leave lasting imprints on our energy field. Negative sound vibrations can accumulate over time, creating subtle disruptions that weaken the auric field and lower our overall vibrational state. Protecting our energy field from such vibrations is essential for maintaining balance and vitality. One way to shield ourselves is by using earplugs or noise-canceling headphones in loud, chaotic environments, where harsh or overwhelming sounds could otherwise penetrate and destabilize our energy field. Avoiding prolonged exposure to negative soundscapes, such as harsh or aggressive music, angry conversations, or other discordant noises, also helps preserve the harmony of our energetic body.

In addition to avoidance, sound healing techniques can be employed to actively restore balance and strengthen the energy field. Chanting sacred syllables, such as "Om," or practicing toning—producing elongated, harmonious vocal sounds—can recalibrate the vibrations within your body and auric field. These practices create resonant frequencies that align with higher vibrations, purifying and fortifying your energetic state. Sound healing is not merely a tool for recovery; it is a practice of alignment, a way of attuning yourself to the universal symphony and reclaiming inner harmony.

It is also crucial to recognize the power of the sounds we create ourselves. The words we speak and the thoughts we think are carriers of energy, projecting vibrations into the world around us. Words, whether spoken aloud or silently in the mind, act as energetic seeds, capable of influencing not only your state of being but also the energetic environment of those you encounter. Negative or destructive language can reverberate through your energy field, creating disharmony within yourself and those nearby. On the other hand, positive, uplifting words can elevate your vibrational state and promote harmony in your surroundings.

By choosing words and thoughts that align with positivity and truth, you actively shape a supportive energetic environment. This mindfulness extends beyond speech; it includes the tones, inflections, and intentions behind your words. The sound of your voice, when imbued with love, kindness, or encouragement, carries a vibration that can uplift others and enhance your own well-being.

Sound is more than a sensory experience—it is a tool of creation, a force that molds and influences the vibrational fabric of existence. By cultivating awareness of the sounds you expose yourself to and the sounds you emit, you take an active role in shaping your energy field and aligning with higher frequencies. This practice not only strengthens your connection to the divine but also enhances your ability to move through life with balance, grace, and harmony.

Mind Control

Your life is an ongoing and profound thought process, one that holds the boundless potential for enlightenment. Every thought you have is part of an expansive journey—a descent into understanding and an ascent into higher comprehension. Through descending, you explore the depths of experience, learning the intricacies of duality and materiality. By ascending, you rise above these limitations, gaining a broader and more unified perspective. This journey leads to an evolution of consciousness, where you transcend the confines of the physical realm and emerge as an enlightened being, often referred to as the Sun of God—a radiant reflection of divine wisdom and light.

It is crucial to understand that your thoughts possess immense creative power. Just as the mental universe perpetually expands, giving rise to new universes and worlds, so too do your thoughts continuously shape and manifest new realities for you. Each thought is a seed of potential, a blueprint for the reality you experience. By consciously taking command of your mind and authentically thinking your own thoughts, you gain mastery over your life. This mastery is not about controlling every circumstance but about aligning your inner world with your highest purpose. When you achieve this alignment, your thoughts become intentional and precise, unlocking the ability to manifest a life that resonates with truth and harmony.

Mental mastery is the gateway to profound transformation. It brings you into alignment with your soul's purpose, connecting you to the flow of divine will. As you increasingly attune yourself to divine will, your thoughts are no longer solely governed by personal desires or external influences. Instead, they are guided by the supreme Godhead, the infinite intelligence that permeates all existence. In this state of alignment, your mind becomes a vessel for divine wisdom, allowing you to navigate life with clarity, purpose, and grace.

Recognize that your thoughts are not random—they are tools of creation. Each one carries the potential to build, transform, or expand your reality. To control your mind is to control the reality you experience. This control requires discipline, awareness, and an unwavering commitment to truth.

It involves observing your thoughts, questioning their origins, and redirecting them when they deviate from your higher purpose. By doing so, you free yourself from the limitations of reactive thinking and step into the realm of conscious creation.

As you progress on this path, you will notice that your mind becomes increasingly attuned to the divine frequencies of the universe. This attunement is not about surrendering control; rather, it is about co-creating with the divine. In this partnership, your thoughts become aligned with the greater flow of universal intelligence, and your life becomes a reflection of this harmony. Through this alignment, you embody the essence of the Sun of God, radiating light and wisdom into the world.

Mastering your mind is not just a personal journey—it is a spiritual imperative. It is the means by which you transcend the illusions of duality and materiality, awakening to the truth of your divine nature. The process of mental mastery is the process of self-realization, a journey of ascending into higher consciousness and descending with greater understanding, creating a life that is in perfect alignment with the divine.

Inanimate Objects

All things, even inanimate objects, possess consciousness because the Creator is present within them. However, their level of interaction with the universe differs from that of human beings, who possess an active, dynamic connection with creation. While objects may carry energy or serve as symbolic reflections of their environment, it is essential to recognize their role as tools, not masters. We must stop allowing inanimate objects to manipulate our emotions or negatively influence our thought patterns. To do so is to surrender our creative power and diminish our potential for mastery.

True mastery begins with taking command of your mind, ensuring that your thoughts and emotions remain unaffected by the presence or absence of material things. Inanimate objects have no power over you unless you grant them significance. Whether it's the loss of a cherished item or the allure of material possessions, these objects must not dictate your state of being. As masters of the universe, we are called to be unwavering, maintaining control over both the objects we interact with and the creative space we inhabit.

Mastery also involves recognizing your role as the architect of your inner reality. The mind is the ultimate tool for shaping your experiences. When you control your mind and direct it with intention, you entangle with the universe in alignment with your will. Your thoughts, like blueprints, construct the reality you inhabit. By consciously designing your inner space, you set the foundation for a harmonious and beautiful manifestation in the external world.

The metaphysical mind does not fixate on the appearance of things as they are but instead envisions what it desires to see—and by doing so, brings it into being. This creative act is not about denial of the current reality but about transcending it through focused intention and belief. You are not bound by the limitations of the material world; your mind can mold, reshape, and redefine what you experience.

To achieve this, you must cultivate clarity and discipline. Instead of reacting to objects or circumstances, you consciously engage with them, assigning them meaning only when it serves your higher purpose. This deliberate relationship with the material world reinforces your mastery, allowing you to use objects as tools for growth rather than obstacles to peace.

By mastering your mind and reclaiming your creative power, you align yourself with the infinite potential of the universe. Your thoughts become the seeds of reality, and your inner vision becomes the force that shapes the external world. Let your mind reflect the beauty and harmony you wish to see, and trust that the universe will respond in kind.

Coming to Terms

Coming to terms with the inevitability of physical death is one of the most profound steps in understanding the nature of existence. Death, as we perceive it, is not an end but a transformation—a shedding of the old, much like removing worn clothing. While the physical body ceases to function, life itself persists in a new and different form. The essence of who we are, our soul, is eternal, transcending the physical limitations of this plane.

Consider the burning of a candle. Once it is burned, we no longer call it a candle, yet its essence—its light, warmth, and energy—continues in another form. The wax melts, the flame disappears, but the energy released is neither destroyed nor lost. Similarly, our physical body is but an avatar, a vessel for the soul during this earthly journey.

When we depart from it, we do not cease to exist; we assume a new state of being. The soul remains fully alive, vibrant, and free, no longer called by the name we knew but by a new one aligned with its next stage of existence.

Though it can be deeply painful to lose someone we love, it is important to shift our perspective on death. Mourning, while natural, often generates low-frequency energy that can weigh heavily on both us and the departed. Instead of lingering in sorrow, we can honor their journey by sending prayers, love, and high aspirations for their next phase of existence. These elevated frequencies support and uplift their soul as they transition to a new realm. By doing so, we not only offer them peace but also find solace in knowing they are no longer bound by the struggles of the physical world.

Death, in its truest sense, is a return to freedom. The soul, no longer confined by the limitations of the body, embarks on a new chapter of its eternal journey. By coming to terms with this truth, we can face the inevitability of physical death with grace, knowing that it is not an end but a transformation. The connection we share with those who have passed transcends the physical plane, allowing us to feel their presence in new and meaningful ways.

In accepting the continuity of life beyond the physical, we free ourselves from the fear of death. This understanding allows us to celebrate the lives of those who have transitioned, knowing that their essence endures, vibrant and eternal. Through love, prayer, and high-frequency energy, we honor their journey while strengthening our own connection to the infinite cycle of existence.

Mental Hygiene

Transforming negative thoughts into their positive counterparts is a deeply transformative practice that can elevate your entire state of being. This is not merely about thinking positively but about actively reshaping your inner landscape to align with higher vibrations. A clear purpose in life acts as a guiding light, naturally purifying various aspects of your lifestyle. When you cultivate purpose, you align your actions, thoughts, and energy with a meaningful direction, bringing harmony and clarity to the mind.

Engaging in practices like meditation helps cleanse and center the mind, while immersing yourself in positive and insightful reading materials promote self-exploration and growth. Books and teachings that encourage introspection and connection with your higher self serve as tools for maintaining mental hygiene. However, it is important to remember that the goal is not to become burdened by excessive intellectualism or knowledge for its own sake. Instead, the purpose is to harness personal power and use knowledge as a means of empowerment.

Knowledge itself is a force, a convergence of thought forms that shape our understanding of the world. Even the word "information" reveals its deeper nature: it is "in" "formation"—the alignment of thoughts and ideas into a coherent structure. When we consciously choose what information we absorb, we shape our mental and spiritual realities in ways that align with our higher purpose.

To reflect the higher self, maintaining a clear and untainted mind is essential. Contamination of the mind occurs when it becomes inundated with random, conflicting, or overwhelming thoughts.

These distractions weigh down the spirit and obscure the clarity needed for true self-expression. Mental clutter, whether it arises from external influences or internal conflicts, creates distortions that prevent you from seeing and embodying the divine essence within.

To transcend the limitations of the mind, it is necessary to release attachment to thoughts altogether, whether they are positive or negative. While positive thoughts may uplift, attachment to any thought binds you to the mental plane, keeping you within its cycles. True freedom and liberation come from cultivating a state of neutrality and impartiality—a space where the mind is neither reactive nor possessive of its contents. This state allows you to observe thoughts without judgment or attachment, enabling you to transcend the mind's limitations and access a deeper connection with the higher self.

Neutrality is not indifference; it is the ability to navigate life with clarity and balance, unshaken by external circumstances or internal fluctuations. In this state of mental purity, you reflect the light of the higher self with precision and grace, embodying the divine wisdom that lies within. By practicing mental hygiene, you create a sacred space within your mind where higher knowledge can flow freely, shaping your life and aligning you with your ultimate purpose.

Sexual Imagery

In the modern digital landscape, platforms like Instagram and TikTok thrive on captivating imagery, drawing millions of users into an endless stream of visual content. These images, particularly those of a provocative or sexual nature, interact deeply with the mind and body, triggering a cascade of physiological and chemical responses. The simple act of engaging with such imagery can release neurotransmitters like dopamine, which is associated with pleasure and reward, as well as stress hormones such as cortisol and adrenaline. This demonstrates the profound power of the mind to influence the body's chemistry, even in the absence of physical interaction.

Remarkably, the mind's capabilities extend to the realm of sexual pleasure itself. It is possible to experience orgasmic sensations purely through mental imagery, proving that the mind is an extraordinary orchestrator of chemical and electromagnetic processes. These processes can generate profound feelings and sensations, many of which remain undocumented or poorly understood. By intentionally focusing one's attention on sources of satisfaction and deliberately channeling the mind's faculties, an individual can harness this power to manifest states of bliss, aligning their internal reality with their desired experience. This underscores the mind's creative potential, offering opportunities for both liberation and mastery over one's emotional and sensory landscape.

However, for males especially, it is important to consider the implications of excessive exposure to sexual imagery, particularly the depictions of partially or fully unclothed women that saturate social media platforms. From a metaphysical perspective, this constant exposure—without active participation in intimacy—has the potential to cultivate states of passivity or submission. This phenomenon arises because the mind, which is intimately connected to the body, absorbs and reacts to visual stimuli in ways that shape one's psychological and energetic framework.

The repeated and unbalanced consumption of such imagery creates a disconnect between intention and action, reducing personal agency. This can weaken the ability to assert desires or take active roles in intimate experiences, as the brain begins to associate fulfillment with passive observation rather than active engagement. The energetic implications are profound: the individual's personal power is diminished as their energy is subtly siphoned by external stimuli, leaving them in a state of dependency on the very imagery that triggered these responses.

At the scientific level, this dynamic is rooted in the complex interplay between the mind and body. The human brain, a remarkable nexus of consciousness and perception, processes visual stimuli in intricate ways. When exposed to repeated sexual imagery, the brain initiates a cascade of neural responses that alter psychological patterns over time. These patterns can manifest as reduced confidence, a lack of decisiveness, or even a diminished ability to connect authentically in real-life relationships. Metaphysically, this represents a misalignment of the energy centers, particularly those tied to personal empowerment, creativity, and intimacy.

The overconsumption of sexual imagery places the individual in a passive energetic state, where they become more of an observer than a participant in their own experiences. This passivity affects not only intimate relationships but also the broader sense of self, reducing the individual's ability to assert control over their desires and actions. It is a subtle erosion of personal empowerment, where the constant intake of external stimuli overrides the internal will.

To counter this, one must cultivate awareness and intentionality. By consciously regulating exposure to sexual imagery and redirecting attention toward meaningful and active experiences, it becomes possible to reclaim personal agency and restore energetic balance. Practicing mindfulness, engaging in fulfilling relationships, and focusing on self-empowerment are key steps in transcending the passive states induced by overexposure. The goal is to master the mind's interaction with stimuli, transforming external influences into opportunities for growth and alignment rather than sources of disempowerment.

Ultimately, this awareness allows individuals to reconnect with their creative and intimate energies in authentic ways, leading to deeper fulfillment and a strengthened sense of self. The power of the mind is immense, and by directing it consciously, one can transcend the limiting effects of external imagery and harness its true potential for personal and spiritual growth.

Do's and Don'ts

At the bare minimum, meditate. Make meditation a cornerstone of your life. You don't need to follow a specific religion or adhere to intricate traditional beliefs to progress on your spiritual path. Just learn how to meditate. Meditation is the practice that will unlock the clarity and focus necessary for mastering your mind. Developing your ability to concentrate is crucial because concentration is the most important tool in gaining control over your thoughts. A lack of concentration allows the mind to run wild, scattering your energy and creating unnecessary problems. A disciplined mind, on the other hand, is productive and aligned with your purpose.

When you tame your wild thoughts, you'll notice a remarkable shift: the things you once chased after will now chase after you. This is the correct position to be in—the mental platform where you stand firmly in alignment with divine flow. Surrender your will to God, trusting that God's will for you is the ultimate happiness, health, and abundance. Affirm this daily: *"I am willing to do the will of God, and I trust that God's will is the ultimate right thing for me."* When you align with divine will, all that you dream of will seek you out, eager to manifest in your life. The key is this surrender, which is not about giving up control but about harmonizing with the ultimate source of wisdom and creation.

Begin with the Body

One effective way to initiate the process of mind control is to start at the foundational level—by exerting influence over the body. Your body is deeply intertwined with your mind, and its impulses often dictate your thoughts and actions. Techniques such as purifying the body and regulating the impulses of the glands are essential first steps. Pay particular attention to the influence of the sexual and digestive organs, as these hold significant sway over your thoughts, emotions, and energy. When your life is dominated by the impulses of these organs, your ability to concentrate and ascend to higher levels of consciousness is limited.

To truly direct your thoughts toward specific chakras, you must first gain mastery over the physical body. You cannot command your energy centers if your glands and senses control you.

By reducing the degree to which the body dictates your actions, you begin to free yourself from its dominance. This liberation is a critical step in the journey toward self-mastery and spiritual growth.

Transcend Bodily Impulses

To ascend to higher consciousness, it is essential to transcend the dominance of bodily elements. Begin by observing how often your actions are driven by physical desires or emotional reactions tied to your glands and organs. Awareness is the first step in loosening their grip. Practice discipline in your diet, your habits, and your responses to urges. Through this discipline, you begin to assert your authority over the body, reclaiming the energy that is often scattered by unregulated impulses.

When you achieve mastery over your physical self, you open the door to chakra-directed thought. This means intentionally focusing your mental energy on specific energy centers to align, balance, and activate them. By gaining control over your body, you lay the foundation for deeper spiritual work, allowing your mind to rise above distractions and focus on the higher realms of consciousness.

The Path to Mastery

Establishing command over the body's functioning is not just a physical process—it is the groundwork for governing the mind. The body and mind are deeply interconnected; by taming one, you strengthen the other. As you gain mastery over the body, you create space for the mind to operate with greater clarity and intention.

This enhanced control allows you to delve into the metaphysical realms of energy centers, expanding your consciousness and aligning your will with divine purpose.

Ultimately, this journey begins with small, deliberate steps. Meditate daily. Cultivate concentration. Observe and regulate the body's impulses. With each practice, you build the foundation for self-mastery, creating a harmonious alignment between your body, mind, and spirit. In this state, you move closer to your highest potential, standing firmly in the flow of divine will, ready to create a life of profound meaning and fulfillment.

Technique for Trauma

Addressing trauma requires a gentle yet powerful approach, one that acknowledges the pain without allowing it to dominate your emotional or mental state. A simple yet transformative technique is to engage in silent and peaceful meditation. This practice creates a sacred space within your mind, enabling you to process the trauma from a place of clarity and detachment.

Begin by finding a quiet, comfortable place where you can meditate without interruptions. Close your eyes, take slow and deliberate breaths, and allow your mind to settle. Focus on clearing your thoughts and entering a state of calm. Spend approximately 20 minutes in this meditative state, allowing your inner stillness to grow. This time prepares your mind to address the trauma without becoming overwhelmed by it.

Once you feel centered and grounded, bring the traumatic event to your mind's eye. Visualize it clearly, as if you are observing it on a screen or from a distance. The key here is detachment—do not react emotionally or relive the event. Instead, observe it as a neutral witness, as though you are watching someone else's story. Take approximately five minutes to calmly examine the trauma from all angles. Look at it objectively, analyzing its details without judgment or fear. This detached observation helps you to disarm the emotional charge the trauma holds over you.

When your observation is complete, consciously release the traumatic event from your consciousness. Envision it dissolving or floating away, leaving your mind clear and unburdened. Affirm to yourself that you are no longer defined or controlled by this experience. Say silently or aloud, *"I release this event from my mind and my heart. It no longer has power over me."*

This practice may need to be repeated over time, as deeper layers of the trauma may surface for processing. With each session, you will notice that the emotional grip of the trauma weakens, gradually freeing you from its hold. What once caused pain and turmoil now becomes a neutral memory, devoid of the power to disrupt your peace.

This technique works because it addresses trauma at its energetic root. Traumatic events often leave imprints on your energetic and emotional bodies, causing blockages or disruptions in your natural flow of energy. By observing the trauma without reacting, you neutralize the energetic charge it holds. The act of conscious release removes this blockage, restoring harmony to your energy field and mind.

Over time, this practice brings profound liberation, allowing you to affirm a new reality. You begin to embody strength, clarity, and a deeper awareness of your resilience. Trauma, once a source of suffering, becomes a stepping stone to greater self-awareness and empowerment.

As you move forward, embrace the awareness that you are more than your experiences. Trauma may shape parts of your journey, but it does not define your essence. By mastering techniques like this, you reclaim your power, opening the door to healing and transformation.

The Fiddle

Many individuals are often too uncertain or conflicted about their own sense of self to be directing significant energy toward attacking the image or reputation of others. Their internal ambivalence, stemming from unresolved feelings or insecurities, often overshadow any inclination of their engagement in harmful actions. This inner conflict serves as a reminder that the priority lies within resolving one's own ambivalence and achieving inner clarity rather than directing negativity outward. Without harmonizing these conflicting energies, individuals remain caught in a cycle of projection, inadvertently fueling the systems of control that exploit their unresolved inner turmoil. This unresolved ambivalence, however, does not merely remain an internal struggle. It finds its way outward, as those plagued by their own insecurities and inner conflicts often project their discord onto the world. In doing so, they construct systems of manipulation and control, embedding their own unresolved fears into the very fabric of society. It is this projection of inner imbalance that has given rise to the parasitic elite and their carefully orchestrated matrix of deception.

The parasitic elite have mastered the art of manipulation through the concept of money—a fiat currency devoid of intrinsic value. By leveraging this construct, they ensnare individuals within a carefully orchestrated financial matrix. This matrix is not merely economic but psychological, as it embeds the idea of scarcity into consciousness, anchoring individuals in survival-based thinking tied to their base instincts and lower chakras. Through this illusion, a poverty mindset takes root, shaping thoughts and beliefs to accept limitation as a fundamental reality. Trapped in this paradigm, individuals find their energy focused solely on securing basic needs, stifling their ability to advance spiritually, mentally, or creatively. Stripped of access to wealth—not just financial but also energetic—due to a lack of information, opportunities, or tools, they remain confined to the lower rungs of existence, unable to transcend the confines of the matrix.

This adversary, through calculated propaganda, has strategically obstructed humanity's intuitive perception of truth and reality. By severing the connection to higher mental faculties—such as remote viewing, telepathic abilities, and profound intuitive insights—the adversary creates a distorted reality tunnel. These faculties, which are essential for transcending the limitations of the physical world, are systematically suppressed. Propaganda, coupled with manipulative constructs, ensures that individuals remain tethered to lower frequencies of thought, unable to access the expanded awareness necessary for liberation.

The methods employed by this adversary are diverse and far-reaching. Religious frameworks, often dogmatic in nature, serve to impose rigid mental structures. Educational systems, designed more for conformity than enlightenment, dampen curiosity and independent thought. Social media algorithms perpetuate distraction and comparison, pulling attention away from meaningful self-reflection. Institutionalized brainwashing, linguistic constructs, and psychological manipulation weave an intricate web that ensnares the mind, restricting its natural expansive tendencies. The result is a population mentally subdued, less capable of challenging the imposed matrix and reclaiming their higher faculties.

It is important to understand that the absence of a mental equivalent on the mental plane results in the absence of a physical equivalent on the physical plane. What exists in the mind manifests in reality, and when imagination and mental perspective are obstructed, physical, mental, and spiritual imprisonment follow. This principle reveals the true depth of the adversary's attack: by controlling imagination, they control potential. A mind without freedom cannot create a reality beyond its imposed boundaries.

Conversely, when the physical body is imprisoned, whether by poverty or oppressive systems, the potential of the mind becomes restricted as well. Poverty, as a physical manifestation of lack, is not merely an economic condition but a deliberate assault on the mental and spiritual well-being of individuals. It binds them in survival mode, diverting energy away from higher pursuits and deeper awareness. Poverty becomes a dual affliction—constraining the physical and launching a direct attack on the psyche, instilling feelings of helplessness and limiting the capacity to dream, imagine, or aspire.

To transcend this construct, one must reclaim their mental sovereignty. Recognize that the physical plane is a reflection of the mental plane and begin to dismantle the scarcity mindset from within. By liberating the mind from imposed limitations, you open pathways to abundance, creativity, and freedom. Imagination, unshackled, becomes the force that reclaims your reality, dissolving the false constructs imposed by the adversary.

The antidote lies in reactivating your higher faculties and realigning with the truth of your infinite potential. Begin with clarity of thought, purposeful imagination, and the deliberate rejection of scarcity-driven beliefs. In this reclamation of mental and spiritual power, the adversary's control fades, and the natural harmony of creation restores itself. The mind, free and expansive, becomes the architect of a liberated existence.

Third Codex

SpellBreaker

All phenomena within the universe possess inherent vibrations, and when these vibrations achieve a harmonious rhythm, the fundamental building blocks of creation align into a vibrational configuration. At first glance, it may appear as though everything originates from chaos, as the energetic fields and vibrating elements seem elusive. However, hidden within this perceived chaos lies an unimaginable reservoir of energy, waiting to be projected into the fabric of spacetime. Once projected, the **law of rhythm** orchestrates this energy into order, creating structure and form within the vibrational field. As the process gains momentum, nature solidifies the initial outpouring, transforming potential energy into manifested reality.

Every aspect of creation adheres to distinct rhythms dictated by the universal laws of rhythm and vibration. Actions and thoughts repeated consistently establish unique energy signatures, and creation responds by shaping and giving form to these signatures. This interplay ensures that what begins as an intangible vibration eventually manifests as a tangible and enduring reality.

It is vital to recognize that nothing can truly be destroyed; all things are merely transformed. The ultimate substance —**The Creator**—is eternal and inviolable. When the mind engages rhythmically with the universe through thought, it activates the creative forces permeating existence. Thoughts, when given sufficient attention and energy, evolve into forms. These forms become patterns, gaining momentum and influencing the rhythm of creation itself. The universe, responding to these rhythmic vibrations, materializes the momentum generated by thought into tangible reality. Nature, in its wisdom, supplies the atoms and energy required to construct the forms requested by the mind's intentions.

However, distorted or untruthful thoughts disrupt this natural rhythm, creating chaos and misfortune. Ignorance can be likened to particles of darkness that obscure the light of consciousness. When dark or distorted thoughts are released into the universe, they often return to the individual as ill fortune. Many individuals unknowingly sabotage their lives through unconscious thinking, falsely attributing their challenges to external forces. In truth, much of their suffering is rooted in their own thought patterns. To improve the conditions of life, one must cultivate positive thought forms and radiate selfless love into the world.

The Law of Compensation and Purpose

The **law of compensation** ensures that the energy you emit—whether positive or negative—returns to you in kind. Imagine the profound healing that could occur if we, with pure hearts, became conduits of love, channeling its frequencies to those in need. This noble endeavor, however, requires effort and intention. Many people traverse life without ever seeking to define their purpose, leaving them vulnerable to manipulation by negative entities.

These entities exploit the law of rhythm to construct mental frameworks that confine individuals within repetitive thought patterns. These rhythms, solidified by nature, keep individuals trapped in cycles of limitation and unawareness.

To uncover your purpose, you must break free from these mental constructs. Societal imprints, religious ideologies, financial burdens, and career expectations often obscure your true calling. A simple yet powerful technique to reconnect with your purpose involves quiet meditation. In this state, dismantle the mental constructs that define your personality and desires, asking: *What remains when all barriers are removed? What stirs the depths of my being?* By exploring these questions, you can rediscover your authentic calling—the one thing you are destined to pursue wholeheartedly and soulfully.

Breaking the Cycle

Many individuals fail to actualize their purpose because they neglect the time and effort required for self-awareness. Instead, they become ensnared in survival-driven cycles, shaped by ingrained thought patterns and societal conditioning. Once you identify your true purpose, commit to it with unwavering resolve. Infuse definiteness into every thought and action, knowing that nature solidifies habitual patterns over time. Never entertain the idea of giving up; failure only arises when you succumb to defeat. As long as you persevere, success remains a possibility and failure will forever elude you.

Neutralizing and Breaking Spells

The efficacy of negative spells lies in their rhythmic momentum. To neutralize them, seek equilibrium between opposing polarities. An evil spell can be counteracted by invoking good vibrations, but the ultimate imperviousness lies in traversing the **neutral path**—the middle way. Spells, like all vibrational patterns, are governed by the law of rhythm. To break their hold, one must transcend external distractions and focus inward. Directing your energy toward introspection and alignment with your higher self diminishes your vulnerability to spiritual attacks.

To break free from **subconscious hypnotism**, you must understand the mechanics of **hypnotic rhythm**—the repetitive thought patterns and behaviors that solidify into mental and physical prisons. This requires delving into the depths of your mind—what could be called **mindmatics**—to uncover the root causes of these rhythms. Through affirmations, you can reprogram your mental code, rewriting the narratives that shape your existence.

Guarding Against Energy Vampires

In this journey, it is essential to protect yourself from energy vampires—entities or distractions that siphon your life force. These vampires can take many forms, including technology, which often consumes vast amounts of mental and emotional energy. Remember, **energy follows the mind**; whatever you dwell on becomes the recipient of your energy. By redirecting your focus away from distractions and toward meaningful pursuits, you safeguard your energy and preserve your life force.

The Path to Liberation

Breaking free from hypnotic rhythm requires a multifaceted approach:

1. **Understand the Mechanics of Hypnosis** – Study your mind and identify the rhythms that confine you.
2. **Apply Affirmations** – Use positive affirmations to overwrite limiting beliefs and reprogram your mind.
3. **Guard Your Energy** – Avoid distractions and energy vampires that drain your vitality.
4. **Cultivate Rhythm and Resolve** – Establish a rhythm of thought and action that aligns with your goals and intentions.

By taking these steps, you embark on a transformative journey to reclaim your autonomy, liberate your mind, and safeguard your life force. Through introspection, discipline, and alignment with higher principles, you break the cycle of hypnotic rhythm and become the architect of your reality. Liberation lies in mastering the interplay of rhythm, thought, and energy—a journey that leads to the ultimate freedom of the self.

Karma

Understanding the four elements of nature—fire, air, earth, and water—is the foundation of wisdom. These elements are not merely physical substances; they are the energetic building blocks of our existence. We think, speak, and act within the framework of these elements, and it is impossible to function outside of them on this plane of existence. Immersion in these elements shapes every aspect of our experience. By learning to understand their influence, we take the first step toward growth, control, and the conscious molding of our reality.

As we advance on the path of divine evolution, the natural fire within us transforms into cosmic fire, elevating our being. Cosmic fire is not just an external force—it is **Love** in its purest form, the energy that cleanses and purifies the physical, mental, and spiritual aspects of our existence. This cosmic fire burns away impurities, illuminating the divine essence within. When we align ourselves with this transformative force, we ascend into higher states of consciousness, allowing love to guide our actions and interactions.

The Power of Thought

Thoughts are not abstract or fleeting—they are **things**, tangible in the metaphysical sense, and they carry the power to manifest into physical reality. A well-defined thought, repeated with focus and intent, will inevitably create a replica of itself in the material world. Our thoughts combine with **elementals**, the energetic building blocks that make up the fabric of creation. These elementals seek out similar vibrations throughout the universe, connecting us with other entities who resonate with the same energy.

This process means that our thoughts act as magnets, attracting corresponding energies in others. Negative thoughts attract negativity, while positive thoughts draw positivity.

This is a fundamental law of creation: we attract what we are. When we experience hardship or misfortune, it is often not the result of divine punishment but the manifestation of our own thoughts and actions. Our thoughts are like seeds planted in the fertile soil of the universe, and the fruit they bear reflects the nature of the seeds themselves.

Karma and the Law of Cause and Effect

Karma is not a system of external judgment but an intricate interplay of cause and effect, rooted in the vibrations we emit. The elementals that make up creation seek to combine with others of like kind, manifesting in various forms—friendships, partnerships, business associates, lovers, comrades, and even enemies. Each interaction is a reflection of the energy we have contributed to the universe.

When we fail to cultivate **divine love** within our hearts, we leave ourselves vulnerable to the accumulation of negative karma. Divine love is the ultimate protective force, shielding us from the discordant vibrations of harmful thoughts and actions. Without love, we misuse the divine power entrusted to us, engaging in behaviors that harm others. This misuse of divine energy is seen as the greatest transgression in the spiritual realm.

Karma is also influenced by unfulfilled desires carried over through the process of reincarnation. These desires, combined with negative interactions in this realm, create karmic imprints that shape our future experiences. Engaging in harmful behavior is not just a transgression against others—it is a betrayal of our own divine potential.

Each act of harm sets into motion a cycle of cause and effect that binds us to lower frequencies, delaying our spiritual evolution.

Breaking the Cycle of Karma

To break free from the cycle of karma, it is essential to align with **divine love** and cultivate thoughts and actions that reflect our highest nature. Begin by becoming aware of your thoughts and the energy they carry. Are they aligned with love, truth, and harmony, or do they reflect fear, anger, and resentment? By consciously choosing thoughts that uplift and empower, you transform the elementals within you, attracting positive experiences and relationships.

Engage in practices that purify the mind and heart, such as meditation, prayer, and acts of kindness. Each positive thought and action sends ripples of high-frequency energy into the universe, neutralizing the effects of negative karma and creating a pathway for higher vibrational experiences.

Understand that karma is not a punishment but an opportunity for growth. It is a feedback mechanism that teaches us the consequences of our energy and actions. When approached with this understanding, karma becomes a tool for spiritual refinement, guiding us toward greater self-awareness and alignment with divine principles.

The Ultimate Responsibility

The ultimate responsibility lies in recognizing that we are co-creators of our reality. Engaging in harmful behavior represents a misuse of the divine power we hold, and this misuse has consequences that extend beyond the individual. It affects the collective consciousness, creating ripples that shape the experiences of others as well.

When we act with love, compassion, and integrity, we align with the higher laws of creation, transforming our karma into a force for good. Each moment is an opportunity to sow seeds of positivity, shaping a future rooted in harmony and abundance. By understanding the interplay of thoughts, elementals, and karma, we take charge of our spiritual destiny, stepping into the role of conscious creators and divine beings.

Words of Power

Words are not mere symbols or sounds—they are powerful tools that shape the reality within us and around us. At their core, words carry vibrations, and these vibrations influence the energetic fabric of existence. Since all things are fundamentally composed of energy, the words we speak and think emit frequencies that mold our experiences.

The language we use to describe ourselves and our circumstances plays a pivotal role in the reality we create. Repeated use of negative or limiting language reinforces beliefs that manifest as obstacles, while positive and empowering words invite alignment with our deepest desires and intentions. Words have the ability to sculpt the narratives we live by, influencing our perceptions, beliefs, and emotions. By choosing words with care, we can reshape our internal dialogue and develop a sense of self that is both empowering and aligned with our higher purpose.

Every thought we form is a vibration, and every word we utter carries that vibration into the world. These vibrations interact with the energy fields around us, creating ripple effects that extend far beyond what we can see. It is our responsibility to infuse our words with the correct frequencies, ensuring they uplift, heal, and inspire. The tones we use resonate deeply within us, vibrating in the king's chamber of our being and permeating our energetic field with their essence. Whether constructive or destructive, positive or negative, every word influences the mind-body field, guiding us toward health or disease, prosperity or poverty, creation or destruction.

The Planetary Impact of Words

On a larger scale, collective words carry immense power. When negativity is spoken and perpetuated globally, it accumulates into a vast vibratory field that affects not only the energetic environment but also the physical planet itself. These accumulations can manifest as severe weather patterns, geological disruptions, or other catastrophic events. The Earth, a living entity, responds to the vibrations we generate, mirroring the collective consciousness of its inhabitants.

In this light, the role of lightworkers becomes vital. As bearers of divine energy, they are tasked with using words of power to restore balance amidst prevailing negativity. Words imbued with divine frequencies act as healing currents, much like the ancient pyramids scattered across the globe that emanate stabilizing energies into the environment. Each lightworker is a beacon, generating positive vibrations akin to Orgone energy, counterbalancing the destructive frequencies that pervade our world.

The Connection Between Heart and Throat Chakra

It is essential to recognize that access to the throat chakra, the center of verbal expression, is deeply connected to the purification of the heart. Without a purified heart, the throat chakra cannot fully activate, and words spoken from an unpurified state may carry destructive rather than creative power. Every day, consciously or unconsciously, we affirm words that shape and reshape our reality. Spoken affirmations are the architects of the mental universe we inhabit, creating structures of thought that manifest in our lives.

Consider the profound example: *"God said, 'Let there be light,' and there was light."* This demonstrates the creative power of words to bring forth existence. Similarly, our words act as commands to the mental universe, shaping our reality through their vibratory resonance. Whether we speak consciously or unconsciously, this energy follows our intentions and manifests accordingly.

The Power of Positive Speech

Recognizing that our journey through life is one of perfection, growth, and illumination, we must monitor our speech with care. Positive words and positive thinking are inseparably linked, each reinforcing the other. Through our spoken words, we have the ability to create, heal, curse, and bless. By speaking positively to ourselves and engaging in a constructive dialogue with our bodies and minds, we take control of our lives and become masters of our destiny.

The power of words extends beyond mere expression—they are tools of transformation. By speaking to ourselves with love, encouragement, and affirmation, we align our energetic fields with the vibration of our highest potential. For example, affirmations such as *"I am healthy, I am abundant, I am aligned with divine will"* not only reinforce these truths within the mind but also radiate them into the universe, attracting the corresponding energy back to us.

Words, Knowledge, and Faith

Words are also the carriers of knowledge, acting as gateways to deeper understanding. As knowledge grows, it instills confidence, which in turn evolves into faith. Faith is not blind belief—it is the union of confidence and understanding, a resonance that aligns us with the divine flow of the universe. Words, when imbued with knowledge, guide us toward greater awareness and mastery, enabling us to access the deeper truths of existence.

Consider the statement: *"In the beginning was the Word, and the Word was with God, and the Word was God."* This profound truth underscores the divine resonance inherent in all things. Words are not separate from creation—they are the very building blocks of it. Just as the sacred syllable *OM* reverberates ceaselessly, its waves permeating the fabric of existence, so too does the cosmos pulse with harmonious vibration, attuned to the eternal symphony of creation.

Living with Words of Power

To live consciously is to recognize the immense power of words and use them wisely. Speak with intention, knowing that every word shapes your reality. Choose affirmations that align with your highest purpose and infuse your speech with divine frequencies. Remember that the mental universe responds to your directives, and through words, you possess the ability to create a life of growth, health, and prosperity.

Let your words be a reflection of your higher self, a channel for divine light. Speak to heal, to bless, and to uplift, knowing that the energy you send into the world will return to you amplified. In doing so, you honor the divine gift of speech and step into your role as a co-creator of the universe.

Positive Affirmation

I embrace the profound understanding that I have been entrusted by **THE ALL**, the universal consciousness, to receive magnificent blessings in my life. **THE ALL**, in its infinite wisdom, has created a universe of abundance where all things are plentiful. As a conscious being, I am the fortunate recipient of boundless love that permeates every aspect of existence. With this awareness, I open myself to the abundant flow of love, allowing it to manifest in all areas of my life. I am receptive to the love that comes from within me and from the world around me. I attract and embrace love in its various forms, be it love for myself, love from others, or love for all beings and the universe itself. In this state of receptivity and gratitude, I align myself with the divine flow of love, and I experience the magnificent blessings that it brings. I am grateful for the love that enriches my life and for the continuous support and abundance that **THE ALL** bestows upon me.

Fourth Codex

The Platform

Thought, second only to the power of love, holds immense influence in shaping our lives. Our thoughts possess the remarkable ability to transform the trajectory of our existence, altering the conditions we experience and aligning us with abundance, prosperity, and well-being. The journey toward mastery begins with recognizing the profound role thought plays in the creation of reality.

To fully harness this power, it is essential to clear the mind of external influences and preconceived beliefs imposed upon us through religion, education, environment, and past experiences. These influences, while often subtle, create filters that obscure our perception and distort our ability to access higher truths. By consciously clearing the mind of these thought impressions, we create a receptive state—a fertile ground where new understanding can take root.

The mind naturally seeks to attach itself to thoughts, constantly craving observation, analysis, and connection. But in learning to maintain a receptive state of mind, we cultivate **intuition**—the gateway to knowledge and truth. Intuition allows us to bypass the clutter of conditioned thinking and directly access the Source of all wisdom.

The Source as Truth and Knowledge

The Source, often referred to as the ultimate reality or divine essence, is synonymous with Truth and Knowledge. These are not separate concepts but two aspects of the same divine principle. Truth represents the fundamental, unchanging principles that govern creation—universal laws that transcend subjective interpretations and cultural biases. Knowledge, by contrast, is the awareness and understanding of these truths, the insights that guide our perceptions and actions.

Within the Source, Truth and Knowledge are inseparable. They flow together in perfect harmony, forming the ultimate reservoir of wisdom and divine consciousness. When we align ourselves with the Source, we tap into this boundless wellspring of understanding, allowing it to permeate our being and guide our lives. This alignment is not passive but an active process of surrendering the ego, clearing the mind, and attuning to the higher vibrations of divine wisdom.

To align with the Source is to recognize that wisdom and understanding arise from unity with the divine essence. In this state, we can explore the depths of Truth, gaining profound insights that expand our awareness and bring us closer to the essence of existence. Through this connection, we experience spiritual growth, an expanded perception of reality, and a deeper resonance with the Creator's intention.

Spirituality vs. Religion

It is important to understand the distinction between spirituality and religion. Spirituality is inherent to human nature—it is the essence of our being and our connection to the divine. Religion, on the other hand, serves as a framework designed to facilitate spirituality, often providing structure and guidance for those seeking the divine. However, true spiritual alignment transcends the boundaries of religion, enabling us to embody our divine essence and recognize our role within the universal laws of creation.

Surrendering to the Source aligns us with our spiritual essence, allowing us to access higher truths and realities. This surrender is not an act of submission but a realization of our interconnectedness with the divine. As we evolve spiritually, we move beyond the idea of servitude and toward an understanding of co-creation with the divine, embodying the truth that we are both creators and manifestations of the universal laws.

Mastering the Mind

To effect meaningful change in our lives and in the collective reality, we must first attain mastery over our own minds. This mastery involves clearing away the inherited notions, beliefs, and perspectives imposed upon us by external sources—family, friends, society, and even books. While these influences often shape our understanding of the world, true liberation arises when we free ourselves from their grip and begin to see reality as it truly is.

Mastering the mind requires a commitment to self-awareness and self-discipline. As we detach from external conditioning, we create space for intuition and direct perception to flourish. This clarity enables us to reconnect with our true nature and purpose, answering fundamental questions about our identity and destiny. Only by understanding ourselves can we contribute to the collective effort of co-creating a reality aligned with divine principles.

Discovering Truth

The pursuit of truth is a deeply personal journey, one that relies on our own faculties of observation, reasoning, and intuition. While there are guides and teachings that can illuminate the path, the ultimate responsibility lies within each individual to seek their own truth. This self-discovery leads to a genuine understanding of existence and a profound connection to the Creator.

Cultivating a contemplative mindset is essential for this process. By maintaining an open and curious posture, we create the conditions necessary for psychic development, allowing us to tap into deeper levels of consciousness and understanding. Coupled with an attitude of love for life and its manifestations, we establish a harmonious connection with the divine mind—a connection that grants us enlightenment according to our unique path.

Aligning with Purpose

Every individual possesses a unique purpose, a trajectory that is theirs alone to follow. Through introspection and self-exploration, we uncover the answers to life's fundamental questions: *Who am I? What am I? Where am I headed?* Embracing these inquiries with sincerity empowers us to embark on a transformative journey of self-discovery, aligning ourselves with our true purpose.

The act of alignment is both personal and universal. As individuals, we must cultivate mastery over our thoughts, emotions, and intentions. Collectively, we must unite with shared purpose and vision to reshape the fabric of our reality. By aligning with the Source, we become active participants in the conscious evolution of ourselves and the world around us, creating a reality that reflects divine wisdom, harmony, and love.

The Journey of Self-Realization

The journey to self-realization is not without its challenges. It requires us to confront the limitations imposed by societal conditioning and inherited beliefs. Yet, as we clear these mental constructs and cultivate a state of openness, we unlock the vast potential within us. The connection to the Source reveals the profound truths that lie beyond the surface of existence, guiding us toward a life of purpose, fulfillment, and divine alignment.

Let us each commit to this journey, embracing the power of thought, the wisdom of intuition, and the guidance of the divine. In doing so, we reclaim our role as co-creators of reality, aligning with the universal rhythm of growth, enlightenment, and transformation.

Internal Ecosystem

When we embark on the exploration of our physical anatomy—examining our teeth, digestive system, and innate inclinations—we uncover profound insights that highlight our potential as beings capable of elevating consciousness through intentional dietary choices. Upon observation, it becomes apparent that human anatomy bears little resemblance to that of carnivorous or herbivorous animals. However, striking similarities emerge when we compare our physiological makeup to frugivorous creatures. Our teeth structure, digestive tract, and even the way our senses interact with nature align closely with those of fruit-eating species.

Consider how our senses naturally guide us toward nourishment in its purest form. In a natural environment, the sight, smell, and texture of ripe fruits hanging from trees evoke a visceral sense of pleasure and appeal. This instinctual attraction to fruits contrasts sharply with the sensory experience of raw meat. It is essential to differentiate between seasoned, cooked meat and the raw, unembellished reality of flesh and blood. For instance, if you've ever visited a butcher's shop, the smell alone is unlikely to inspire feelings of appetite or joy. These observations point to an undeniable alignment between our physiology and a fruit-based diet, suggesting that such a diet may be an integral component of our journey toward heightened consciousness.

By aligning our dietary choices with our natural design and instinctual inclinations, we unlock profound benefits. Fruits, as nature's perfect food, harmonize with our true essence, nourishing both our physical bodies and our energetic fields.

The Vibrational Impact of Food

The food we consume has a direct and undeniable impact on our physical, emotional, and energetic bodies. Every substance emits its own unique vibrational frequency, which interacts with our own. When we consume foods with lower frequencies—such as meat or processed substances—they can lower our vibrational state, impeding our ability to resonate with higher energies.

Our DNA, the sacred blueprint of our being, carries memory. This memory is sensitive to the energetic imprints of the substances we consume. When we ingest animal proteins, we may unknowingly introduce frequencies tied to the traumas and experiences of the animals. This energetic residue can influence our emotional and mental states, potentially lowering our vibrational frequency and creating disharmony within us.

From a metaphysical perspective, the Divine Creator, in infinite wisdom, has already provided everything we need for sustenance and growth. Fruits, in their simplicity and abundance, resonate with the higher frequencies that elevate our consciousness. These water-rich foods, aligned with the cosmic currents that flow through the universe, harmonize with our bodies, which are themselves composed largely of water. In essence, our physical form is an extension of these cosmic currents, and consuming foods that reflect this harmony allows us to align with the divine rhythms of creation.

The Case for a Fruit-Centered Diet

Fruits are nature's gift, brimming with life force, nutrients, and vibrational energy. They exist in a dazzling variety of flavors, colors, and textures, ready for us to pluck and enjoy. Unlike foods that require extensive preparation, fruits are complete in their raw form, offering sustenance that is both immediate and optimal for our well-being.

Organically grown, natural fruits provide the healthiest source of nourishment, free from the toxins and distortions introduced by artificial means. By prioritizing fruits in our diet, we reduce our reliance on other, less harmonious food sources and align ourselves with the inherent wisdom of nature. This shift is not merely physical but profoundly spiritual, as the vibrational resonance of fruits supports higher states of being.

Fruits are abundant in water, nutrients, vitamins, and antioxidants that sustain our physical health while also nourishing our energetic fields. Their natural frequencies resonate with our own, facilitating a state of balance and upliftment. By consuming these high-vibrational foods, we harmonize with nature, aligning with the intentions of the Divine Creator and enhancing our spiritual connection.

The Spiritual Dimensions of Food

When we embrace a diet centered around fruits, we are not merely making a physical choice but stepping into alignment with a divine plan. Fruits carry the vibrational frequencies of light and life, frequencies that uplift our consciousness and attune us to the rhythms of the cosmos.

As we nourish ourselves with these divine gifts, we create a ripple effect that extends beyond our physical well-being, influencing our emotional, mental, and spiritual states.

By consuming foods that resonate with higher frequencies, we facilitate a flow of energy that elevates our entire being. This flow enhances clarity of thought, emotional stability, and a sense of spiritual alignment. Fruits, with their abundant water content and natural vitality, serve as a bridge between the physical and the metaphysical, grounding us in health while connecting us to the divine.

The Journey Back to Harmony

The path to spiritual elevation begins with understanding and honoring the profound connection between what we consume and the energy we embody. By prioritizing a diet rich in natural fruits, we align ourselves with the divine intention of the Creator, promoting health, vitality, and harmony. As we harmonize with the higher frequencies emitted by fruits, we experience a profound transformation that resonates across all levels of our being.

This alignment is not just about dietary choice but a deeper commitment to living in harmony with the wisdom of nature. Through this commitment, we honor the gift of life and step into a state of unity with the Source, embracing a journey of growth, clarity, and spiritual illumination.

External Ecosystem

Our living environments hold profound influence over our well-being, state of mind, and energetic alignment. In today's modern world, many homes are constructed using toxic building materials and designed in ways that deviate from the natural harmony of the Earth. It is essential to recognize that architecture, like everything else, carries energy and has an impact not only on our physical health but also on the energetic dynamics of our space and surroundings.

Crowded places, for instance, accumulate dense elemental energies formed by the collective thought forms of the people inhabiting or visiting them. These energies linger in the environment, subtly influencing those within their sphere. This energetic residue, though unseen, can disrupt our personal harmony, leaving us feeling drained or uneasy. It is crucial to remain mindful of these influences and take steps to protect our mental and energetic fields from their effects.

While it may not be practical for everyone to retreat to the wilderness or live in pristine, untouched areas, we can still make intentional choices to create more natural, harmonious living environments. Through conscious design and thoughtful material selection, we can transform our homes into sanctuaries that nurture and elevate our well-being.

Designing with Nature: Materials and Shapes

One way to align our living spaces with natural harmony is by incorporating **natural materials** such as wood, stone, and clay. These materials not only reduce our exposure to harmful toxins but also carry their own unique energies. For example, wood resonates with grounding and stability, while stone embodies strength and endurance. Clay, often overlooked, offers an earthy energy that connects us to the nurturing essence of the planet. Surrounding ourselves with these materials cultivates a sense of grounding, peace, and connection to the Earth.

Natural materials also possess an intrinsic beauty that appeals to our innate desire for harmony and balance. Unlike synthetic materials, which can feel sterile or lifeless, organic materials resonate with life force energy. Choosing furniture made of wood, bamboo, or other natural elements enhances the energetic quality of our homes, creating an atmosphere of warmth and tranquility.

Incorporating **organic and flowing shapes** into home design can further elevate the energetic flow within our spaces. Soft curves, natural patterns, and the deliberate avoidance of sharp angles promote a sense of ease and comfort. These choices align with the principles of **sacred geometry**, a universal language of shape and proportion that governs the flow of energy. When our environments mirror these natural principles, they harmonize with our energy fields, developing peace, creativity, and balance.

The Role of Air, Water, and Nature

Location plays an integral role in the energetic quality of our living spaces. Proximity to fresh air and natural environments is a key factor in maintaining vibrant health. Open fields, mountaintops, and areas near bodies of water provide us with direct access to the revitalizing energies of nature. The expansive energy of the sky, the grounding power of the earth, and the cleansing flow of water all work together to recharge and realign our energy fields.

Even in urban settings, we can create microcosms of nature within our homes. **Water and air purification systems** are invaluable tools for improving the quality of the elements we interact with daily. Clean water and fresh air are essential not only for physical health but also for maintaining a high vibrational frequency within our living spaces. These systems help remove toxins and restore the purity of the elements, creating an environment that supports optimal well-being.

Energetic Tools and Enhancements

In addition to natural materials and purified elements, **energetic tools** such as **orgonite** can be employed to balance and harmonize the frequencies within our spaces. Orgonite, often made of a combination of resin, metals, and quartz crystals, is believed to transmute negative energy into positive energy. When placed strategically within the home, orgonite can support a more uplifting and balanced environment, shielding the space from external energetic disruptions.

Similarly, incorporating plants into our living spaces enhances the natural flow of energy. Plants act as living filters, improving air quality while radiating calming, grounding energies. They also provide a direct connection to the natural world, creating a sense of harmony and vitality within our homes.

Creating a Healthy Space

By consciously shaping our living environments to reflect the wisdom of nature, we elevate not only the physical atmosphere but also the energetic and spiritual dimensions of our space. This involves more than just selecting materials and tools—it requires an intentional mindset and a commitment to aligning our homes with the principles of balance and harmony.

Practical Tips for Harmonious Living Spaces:

- **Declutter:** A clutter-free environment allows energy to flow freely, reducing stagnation and promoting mental clarity.
- **Incorporate Natural Elements:** Use wood, stone, clay, and bamboo in your furniture, décor, and construction materials.
- **Use Organic Shapes:** Favor rounded edges and flowing designs over sharp angles to promote a sense of ease and calm.
- **Prioritize Air and Light:** Maximize natural light and fresh air by opening windows regularly and using air purification systems.
- **Integrate Plants:** Add indoor plants to improve air quality and create a direct link to nature.

- **Employ Energetic Tools:** Use orgonite or crystals to balance the energy field of your space.
- **Connect with the Earth:** Incorporate elements such as a small indoor fountain, natural stones, or sand to bring the grounding energy of the Earth indoors.

The Bigger Picture

When we align our living environments with natural principles, we create sanctuaries that support our physical, emotional, and energetic well-being. These intentional spaces nurture a deeper connection to the Earth, reminding us of our interdependence with the natural world. They serve as a foundation for harmony, balance, and spiritual growth, providing the energetic support we need to navigate life's challenges.

In choosing to live in alignment with these principles, we honor not only ourselves but also the Earth, contributing to a collective shift toward greater harmony and sustainability. Let us approach our living spaces with the same care and intentionality we bring to our inner worlds, recognizing that both are reflections of the divine blueprint guiding us all.

Take Action

The pursuit of knowledge is not meant to be an endless accumulation of intellectual concepts, nor should it serve to inflate one's sense of importance. Instead, the true purpose of knowledge is to unlock the immense power that arises from a mind in perfect alignment with higher truth. It is through this alignment that we transition from merely knowing to fully embodying and applying wisdom. In doing so, we move beyond the limitations of theoretical discourse, stepping boldly into the realm of practical manifestation.

True mastery lies not in verbose intellectualism but in the integration of what is known with what is done. Knowledge, in its purest form, demands action—it calls us to bridge the gap between understanding and implementation. A well-informed mind that does not act is like a seed left unplanted, full of potential but ultimately barren. It is through deliberate, purposeful action that we transform knowledge into power, creating ripples that reshape our lives and the world around us.

The Role of Love and the Master Teacher

The foundation of all transformative action begins with cultivating **love** within the heart center. This love is not mere sentimentality but a profound, radiant force that aligns us with divine will and attracts the guidance we need to advance on our spiritual path. When we nurture this love, we create a magnetic field that draws to us the presence of a **master teacher**—a guide who embodies the wisdom we seek and can illuminate the way forward.

The master teacher may manifest in various forms, depending on the needs and readiness of the seeker. For some, this guide is the **higher self**, the divine aspect of their being that transcends the limitations of the ego and offers unfailing wisdom. For others, the teacher may take the form of an enlightened individual—someone who has fully embraced their own higher self and serves as a living example of spiritual enlightenment.

This teacher, whether internal or external, functions as a divine conduit, providing invaluable guidance and assisting the seeker in overcoming obstacles that impede growth. Their presence introduces a structured platform for transformation, offering practical tools, disciplined ways of thinking, and methods for elevating consciousness. They act as a mirror, reflecting the potential within the seeker and encouraging them to rise into alignment with their highest purpose.

The Process of Action

Taking meaningful action requires more than a passive desire for change; it involves active participation in the process of transformation. This begins with a conscious decision to clear the mind, open the heart, and align with the principles of divine love. From this space of alignment, we gain clarity on the steps required to bring our inner knowing into the physical world.

1. **Cultivate Inner Love**: Start by developing a sense of unconditional love within yourself. This love serves as the foundation for all meaningful action, aligning you with the universal flow and preparing you to receive higher guidance.

2. **Seek Guidance**: With love as your anchor, open yourself to the presence of a master teacher. Whether this guide is your higher self or an external mentor, trust that they will provide the insights and tools necessary to advance your journey.

3. **Embody Discipline**: True growth requires discipline and commitment. Embrace the practices, teachings, and processes offered by your teacher with sincerity and dedication. These disciplined ways of thinking and living serve as stepping stones toward your evolution.

4. **Act with Intention**: Every action you take should be infused with intention and purpose. Remember that action is the vehicle through which knowledge is made manifest. Let your deeds reflect the wisdom you hold within.

The Master Teacher's Role

The master teacher does not impose their wisdom but instead facilitates the seeker's journey of self-discovery. They provide the seeker with a series of transformative processes, each designed to peel back the layers of illusion and reveal the truth that lies within. These processes may include meditation, reflection, study, and the cultivation of specific virtues such as patience, humility, and perseverance.

The teacher's role is not to lead but to empower. They guide the seeker to access their own divine nature, helping them to recognize that the answers they seek are already within. The true master teacher serves as a reminder of what is possible, inspiring the seeker to rise into their full potential.

The Courage to Act

Taking action requires courage, for it is through action that we confront the barriers that have held us back. It is easy to remain in a state of passivity, comfortable in the safety of untested knowledge. Yet true growth demands that we step into the unknown, armed with faith and a willingness to embrace the challenges that come with transformation.

Each step we take toward aligning our actions with divine truth brings us closer to realizing our highest potential. This is not a one-time effort but a continuous process of refinement and expansion. As we act, we learn; as we learn, we grow; and as we grow, we align more fully with the universal flow of creation.

Living the Wisdom

The ultimate goal of taking action is not merely to achieve external results but to embody the wisdom we possess. By living in alignment with truth, we become the manifestation of divine principles, radiating love, light, and knowledge in all that we do. This embodiment inspires others to take their own steps toward growth, creating a ripple effect that transforms not only individual lives but the collective consciousness.

In this journey, remember that the true teacher resides within. External guides may illuminate the path, but the power to act, to grow, and to transform lies within you. Trust in your innate wisdom, embrace the process of action, and let your life become a testament to the knowledge and love that flows through you.

You Can't Lead If You Can't See

Symbolically, the central nervous system represents the **tree of life**, its intricate network of branches extending throughout the body like a divine blueprint. At the core of this sacred framework lies the **pineal gland**, often referred to in spiritual traditions as the **lamb of God** or the **crook carried by prophets**. This mysterious gland serves as a spiritual compass, guiding the seeker toward higher realms of perception. In biblical allusions, the **12 glands** of the body symbolize the **leaves on the tree of life**, representing latent potential and the capacity to act as healing agents for the "nation"—a metaphor for the self.

These **12 glands** function as spiritual reservoirs, containing the essence of transformation and divine growth. From them emanate the fruits of spiritual awakening—healing energies and wisdom that offer a profound realization of one's divine potential. However, when the **pineal gland** remains closed or dormant, the individual is limited to the confines of ordinary perception, unable to access the higher frequencies of intuition, insight, and cosmic understanding. Without this expanded awareness, true leadership—whether of self or others—remains incomplete.

Activating the Third Eye

The **activation of the pineal gland**, often called the awakening of the **third eye**, is a pivotal step in transcending mundane reality. This spiritual activation opens the gateway to profound intuitive capabilities and elevated perception. With this expanded vision, the leader gains the ability to perceive the unseen, understand the complexities of the world, and approach situations with clarity and wisdom. It is this heightened state of consciousness that enables one to lead not only from intellect but from insight—a quality that transforms mere guidance into profound influence.

By nurturing the pineal gland through meditation, intentional focus, and pure living, the pathway to greater consciousness becomes clear. This awakening illuminates the intricate dynamics of existence, allowing the leader to operate with broader understanding and elevated purpose. To lead effectively is to see beyond the surface, to understand both the subtle and the manifest, and to embody the wisdom drawn from higher realms.

The Regeneration of the Mind

The mind undergoes a **regenerative process** when spiritual substances from the astral body spill over into the mental body. This overflow, akin to a divine infusion, saturates the mental faculties with elevated energies and qualities. During meditation, as the focus ascends to higher realms, the individual becomes a magnet for these transformative energies, drawing them from the depths of their being.

These energies, through the **spinal cord**, ascend to the **crown of the head**, symbolizing the union of earthly existence with divine consciousness. This process mirrors the ancient principle of **"as above, so below,"** which underscores the profound interconnectedness between the macrocosm and the microcosm. Just as the atoms within our physical form collectively reflect the image of God, so too does the vast expanse of the universe mirror the intricate perfection within us.

By engaging with this regenerative process, the leader not only refines their thought patterns but also aligns their mind with the universal rhythm of creation. This alignment promoting clarity, purpose, and a deeper understanding of the self and the world.

Demonstrating Your Potential

If you truly wish to broaden the horizons of your reality, it is essential to **demonstrate your inherent abilities**. This demonstration is not about boasting or seeking validation but about actively engaging with the world in a way that reflects your unique talents and divine potential. By showcasing your skills, capabilities, and insights, you create a **magnetic force** that attracts opportunities and aligns your reality with your aspirations.

This process of tangible expression not only validates your own potential but also inspires growth and fulfillment. In demonstrating your abilities, you leave a lasting impression on the world, paving the way for an expanded reality that mirrors your inner aspirations.

Action becomes the bridge between the internal and the external, transforming what you know and believe into what you experience. By engaging with the world in meaningful ways, you set into motion the energies that shape your reality, ensuring that your life becomes a reflection of your highest potential.

The Path to Leadership

True leadership begins with sight—the ability to see clearly, to perceive beyond the obvious, and to align with the deeper truths of existence. The activation of the pineal gland and the conscious regeneration of the mind are not merely spiritual practices but essential steps in cultivating the vision required for leadership. By aligning with the divine rhythm, nurturing love in the heart, and expressing your inherent abilities, you not only expand your own reality but also inspire and uplift those around you.

Leadership is not confined to directing others; it is the art of embodying wisdom, clarity, and purpose in a way that naturally influences and guides. To lead is to see—to perceive the interconnectedness of all things and to act from a space of elevated understanding. By embracing this path, you awaken to your role as a co-creator, shaping a reality that reflects the divine potential within and around you.

The Watchful Teacher

Ancient axioms reveal profound wisdom, illustrating the interconnected relationship between readiness and divine timing on the spiritual path. When a student reaches a state of readiness, the universe orchestrates the arrival of a suitable teacher to guide their path. Similarly, when a teacher attains a state of readiness, a master emerges, offering deeper wisdom and illumination. Finally, when the master reaches their pinnacle of readiness, they enter a direct connection with the infinite, allowing the divine presence to unfold within their awareness. This cyclical relationship between readiness and guidance reflects the harmonious interplay between aspiration and the divine.

As students on the journey of life, we share a universal teacher that manifests uniquely for each of us. The teacher does not appear in the same form to everyone; rather, it aligns with the individual's state of awareness and capacity to perceive. Each lesson is tailored to the seeker's current level of development, ensuring accessibility and relevance. This adaptability allows the teacher to serve as a dynamic guide, offering wisdom that resonates deeply with the student's stage of evolution while simultaneously encouraging their growth into higher states of consciousness.

The Witness Within

In the realm of interconnectedness, the witness within me is intrinsically entwined with the witness within you. This sacred witnessing transcends individual boundaries, creating a shared energetic space that unites all living entities. As we interact, my witness observes your essence, just as your witness observes mine. This continuous exchange highlights the importance of presenting oneself authentically, embracing the divinity that resides within us all.

By acknowledging and embodying the role of the witness, we establish a profound connection with the universal observer present in every manifestation of creation—human, animal, plant, and beyond. This awareness creates a deep respect for the interconnected web of existence, urging us to align our actions with the divine rhythm that flows through all beings.

Observing the Mind

To truly govern the mind, one must adopt the role of the witness, actively observing its movements. This act of mindfulness is transformative, instilling a sense of vigilance that aligns the mind with harmony and clarity. Consider how children behave when left unsupervised, often becoming mischievous or unruly. Yet, when they are aware of a watchful presence, they naturally adjust their behavior, becoming more obedient and composed. Similarly, the mind, when left unchecked, tends to wander into chaos, indulging in harmful thoughts or actions. However, when it becomes aware of being observed, it aligns itself with higher order, caution, and care.

By consistently observing the mind, we train it to operate within the framework of discipline and awareness. This practice not only cultivates mental clarity but also creates an inner environment where wisdom and intuition can flourish.

The Mind as a Mirror

Understanding the "Self" requires a metaphorical mirror. Just as you would use a physical mirror to see your face, you require a different type of mirror to perceive your true essence. The mind serves as this reflective surface, revealing the deeper layers of your being. However, like any mirror, the mind must be clear, clean, and calm to provide an accurate reflection. A distorted or clouded mind can only offer a skewed image of the self, obscuring your divine potential.

To glimpse the truth of who you are, the mind must be purified and cultivated. This process involves clearing away the distortions created by attachments, fears, and ignorance. Through consistent practice, you can transform the mind into a pristine instrument capable of revealing your higher self.

The Mind's Influence on the Body

The mind not only reflects the self but also influences the physical body. Your face, in particular, serves as a canvas upon which the state of your mind is painted. A clear and tranquil mind radiates beauty, calmness, and divinity, while a restless or troubled mind manifests tension and disharmony in the physical form. By maintaining mental clarity, you align your inner and outer worlds, allowing your inherent beauty and divine essence to shine through.

The Eternal Self

At your core, you are the eternal Self—pure, immortal, and unchanging. This divine essence is a spark of God, ever-present within you. To fully embrace and embody this truth, the mind must be mastered. An undisciplined mind, prone to restlessness and distraction, obscures your true nature and prevents you from realizing your divine potential. Vigilance and discipline are crucial to cultivating a mind that serves as a faithful ally on your journey.

By strengthening and refining the mind, you unlock its potential as a powerful instrument for growth and transformation. An unruly mind, however, becomes a source of turmoil, perpetually pulling you away from peace and satisfaction. To achieve profound spiritual and personal accomplishments, the mind must be regulated, focused, and aligned with the higher self.

Resurrection of the Mind

The ultimate goal is to attain a state of mental resurrection while still inhabiting the physical plane. This transformation is marked by a shift from ignorance to awareness, a rebirth of the mind that allows you to perceive and embody your divine essence. As the mind ascends to this elevated state, it becomes a conduit for higher energies, drawing wisdom and insight from the infinite.

Through this process, you awaken to the interconnectedness of all creation, recognizing the divine rhythm that underpins existence. By disciplining the mind and aligning it with universal truths, you elevate not only your own consciousness but also the collective consciousness, contributing to the greater harmony of the cosmos.

The Nature in Name

Embedded within the very fabric of existence lies a boundless intelligence that permeates all things. This intelligence is the driving force behind our actions, behaviors, and the unique abilities we manifest. Known by many names across cultures and spiritual traditions, it is synonymous with the essence of creation itself. It is the force that animates us, guiding us to fulfill our individual purposes within the grand design of existence.

Each of us is bestowed with a name that resonates with our intrinsic nature—a name that reflects the consciousness, talents, and spiritual capabilities unique to our being. More than a mere identifier, our name serves as a symbolic representation of our essence. It is a guiding light that reveals the qualities we carry and reminds us of our divine place within the infinite domain of life.

The Universal Language

While human language is deeply tied to cultural identity and personal experience, the universe transcends such divisions. It owns all languages, for they are merely tools for communication, intelligence, and comprehension.

However, the **highest form of language** is not crafted by human tongues but is expressed through the silent yet profound symbols of the natural world—the language of nature itself.

The language of nature speaks to us through its patterns, cycles, and manifestations. Each element, each phenomenon, serves as a symbol of universal truths. By developing a deep understanding of this language, we can unlock the secrets of existence and tap into the universal intelligence that flows through all things. In this profound silence, nature reveals wisdom far greater than words can convey, connecting us to the very source of creation.

Transcending Physical Limitations

Many individuals confine their understanding of themselves to the physical body, viewing it as the ultimate measure of their potential. This attachment to the body imposes limitations, anchoring the mind to a finite reality. Yet, to truly expand consciousness and embrace one's divine nature, it is essential to transcend these physical confines. The body, while a remarkable vessel, is not the totality of our being; it is but a fragment of the infinite self.

By releasing attachment to the body and embracing the concept of **omnipresence**, the mind becomes free to explore infinite possibilities. Through meditative practices and deep introspection, one can dissolve the boundaries of physical limitation and venture into the vast expanses of spiritual reality. In doing so, the mind aligns with the boundless nature of the universe, developing a profound interconnectedness with all that is.

The Universal Law of Mind

At the heart of our spiritual journey lies the aspiration to embody the **universal law of mind**—the principle that governs all existence. This law reminds us that the universe is a reflection of thought and intention. By aligning ourselves with this law, we tap into the limitless potential that exists within us. We realize that we are not separate entities but extensions of the divine mind itself, boundless and eternal.

Truth, in its purest form, transcends the individual. It encompasses the entirety of existence, for it is a manifestation of the whole. When God creates, it does not divide or separate itself but extends itself fully into all of creation. This extension means that we, too, are divine, inseparable from the Creator. The perception of separation from the divine or from the universe is an illusion rooted in our psychology—a veil over our true nature.

Embracing Divine Oneness

To recognize that we are indivisible from the Creator is to embrace the profound truth that we are not merely in the universe; we **are** the universe, expressed in human form. Each of us carries the essence of God, and our journey is to awaken to this realization. By dismantling the illusion of separation, we align with our true nature as extensions of the divine mind.

This alignment allows us to embody the principles that underpin all existence—harmony, unity, and boundless potential. Through this understanding, we dissolve the barriers of ego and limitation, stepping into our roles as co-creators of reality. The question then arises:

What is your name?

Not merely the one you were given at birth, but the name that resonates with the truth of who you are—the name that embodies your essence, your nature, and your divine purpose.

Epigenetic Feelings

Epigenetic memory can be likened to the immune system, a vigilant defender of the body's equilibrium. Just as the immune system identifies and responds to biological threats by producing antibodies with memory, so too does the ancestral memory encoded within our DNA react to environmental cues and stimuli. This deep-seated memory, passed down through generations, functions as a reservoir of wisdom and response patterns, shaped by the experiences of our ancestors.

When the immune system encounters a familiar pathogen, it mobilizes a targeted response based on its memory of past encounters. Similarly, our ancestral DNA, containing the imprints of historical challenges and triumphs, may activate latent responses when faced with similar environmental triggers. These responses are not purely physical but often manifest as emotional and psychological reactions.

In this way, the mind acts as a metaphysical immune system, reacting to threats and challenges that disrupt the equilibrium of our divine essence.

Ancestral Memory and Emotional Responses

The oppressive conditions of the present environment can awaken these ancestral imprints, eliciting feelings that mirror the emotional responses our ancestors once experienced. For example, prolonged stress, societal oppression, or exposure to conditions reminiscent of historical struggles may evoke sensations of depression, anxiety, or a sense of unease. These feelings are not merely personal; they are echoes of the collective memory within us, a reflection of unresolved struggles encoded into the very fabric of our being.

Much like the immune system's response to bacterial or viral intrusions, these emotional reactions serve as a call to action, urging us to restore balance and harmony. However, unlike the physical immune system, which operates autonomously, the mind requires conscious awareness and intentional engagement to address these responses effectively. By understanding the origins of these feelings, we gain the ability to transmute them, turning inherited burdens into opportunities for healing and growth.

The Role of Awareness in Transcendence

To navigate the influence of epigenetic feelings, it is crucial to cultivate a heightened state of self-awareness. Recognizing that these emotions may not originate solely from present circumstances but also from ancestral memory allows us to approach them with compassion and detachment. This perspective shifts the focus from being overwhelmed by emotional responses to understanding their purpose and meaning.

Meditative practices, visualization, and intentional breathwork can serve as tools to reprogram these inherited imprints. By engaging the mind in these practices, we access the deeper layers of consciousness where these memories reside, allowing us to release their hold and transform them into sources of empowerment.

Healing the Ancestral Lineage

When we confront and heal the emotions triggered by epigenetic memory, we are not only addressing our individual experiences but also contributing to the healing of our ancestral lineage. Each time we transmute inherited pain into wisdom and compassion, we ripple these vibrations backward through time and forward into future generations. This act of healing becomes a profound spiritual responsibility, aligning us with the divine essence of renewal and transformation.

In this light, the oppressive conditions of the present can be reframed as opportunities to resolve ancestral struggles.

The depression or discomfort we feel becomes a signal, much like the immune system's response, that something within us requires attention and care. By embracing these feelings with mindfulness and intention, we not only restore balance within ourselves but also contribute to the collective evolution of consciousness.

The Divine Immune System

Just as the immune system protects the body, the mind serves as the immune system of the soul, safeguarding the equilibrium of our divine essence. This metaphysical immune system reacts to disruptions not with antibodies but with thoughts, emotions, and insights, guiding us toward the resolution of internal and external disharmony. When we perceive these reactions as opportunities for growth rather than burdens, we unlock the potential for profound healing and self-realization.

Through this understanding, we come to see that our emotional responses, particularly those rooted in epigenetic memory, are not obstacles but stepping stones. They connect us to the broader narrative of our existence, bridging the experiences of our ancestors with our own journey. By engaging consciously with this process, we transcend the limitations of inherited memory and step into the boundless potential of our true essence.

You Are the Drug

Substances such as drugs possess the capacity to manipulate, stimulate, reduce, or enhance the intricate workings of the human body. Yet, the effects these substances produce are not foreign to us; they are merely external activators of processes that are already encoded within our physiological framework. These substances tap into the body's natural ability to produce specific chemicals and trigger particular responses.

Take dopamine, for instance. Often associated with feelings of pleasure and reward, dopamine can be stimulated by external substances or activities. However, the body itself is the true source of this neurotransmitter, capable of producing it independently of any external influence. **This truth reveals a profound principle: you don't need anything outside of yourself when you master the ability to generate the thought forms that naturally produce these responses.**

The Inner Alchemy of Emotion

Consider the sensation of love, a state where the body undergoes a cascade of chemical transformations. These transformations can manifest as a fluttering sensation in the stomach, often described as "butterflies." It's tempting to attribute this chemistry solely to the presence of another person, but the reality is far more empowering. These feelings originate within the self, activated by the mind and body's response to the emotion of love.

This realization holds immense power. It suggests that the presence of another person is not the sole determinant of our emotional states. Instead, we possess the innate ability to consciously generate these experiences within ourselves. By focusing on the feelings associated with positive emotions—love, joy, gratitude—we can awaken the chemical processes that create these states, independent of external triggers.

The Art of Self-Generated States

This mastery of self-generated emotional states is akin to a form of inner alchemy. By directing your thoughts and cultivating specific emotional patterns, you can tap into the body's inherent capacity to create the sensations and states of fulfillment you seek. This practice is not only transformative but also liberating, as it places the power to cultivate joy, peace, and contentment squarely within your own hands.

Imagine harnessing this power to shift your internal state at will, creating feelings of love, peace, or exhilaration simply by aligning your thoughts and energy. This is the essence of true sovereignty over your well-being— becoming your own healer, your own source of joy, and your own "drug."

Conscious Co-Creation

The implications of this practice extend beyond the self. By consciously generating positive states of being, you contribute to the collective energy field around you. Your internal chemistry, driven by the energy of love, gratitude, or compassion, radiates outward, influencing those you interact with and the environment you inhabit. This ripple effect demonstrates the interconnectedness of all beings and the power each of us holds to shape the world through our internal states.

As you refine your ability to generate these states, you not only improve your own quality of life but also serve as a beacon of positivity and empowerment for others. **You become the catalyst for change, not by seeking external validation or sources, but by embodying the truth that you are the source.**

Reclaiming Your Power

To realize that you are the source of your emotional and chemical states is to reclaim a profound power. It is a recognition that you are not at the mercy of external substances, circumstances, or individuals. Instead, you are the creator of your experience, equipped with the tools and potential to design a life rich in fulfillment, health, and joy.

By embracing this truth, you step into a deeper relationship with yourself—a relationship rooted in awareness, intention, and self-mastery. In this way, you transcend reliance on external substances or triggers, tapping into the boundless well of resources within. You are, and always have been, the source of your own transformation.

Living in Illusion

The concept of illusion is profound and multifaceted, offering various interpretations depending on how we choose to frame our reality. It invites us to reflect deeply on the distinction between living out our dreams and fulfilling our purpose versus being disconnected from our true essence.

From one perspective, **the illusion lies in not living out your dreams and fulfilling your purpose.** This viewpoint suggests that failing to pursue your authentic desires and align with your inner calling can create a life that feels hollow and disconnected. It emphasizes the transformative power of self-discovery, personal growth, and taking aligned action to bring your purpose into reality. When we ignore this calling, we fall into the illusion of a life shaped by external expectations and societal norms, rather than our own truth.

On the other hand, **the illusion may also lie in attachment to external dreams and desires.** This perspective warns of becoming fixated solely on specific outcomes or material achievements, which often leads to disillusionment and dissatisfaction. In this sense, chasing external validation can create a false sense of fulfillment, masking the deeper longing for inner peace and connection to one's true essence. This viewpoint highlights the importance of cultivating inner fulfillment and recognizing that true contentment arises from within, independent of external circumstances.

The Balance Between Dreams and Essence

The tension between these two perspectives invites us to explore an essential question: **What does it mean to live authentically?** Ultimately, the journey to understanding illusion versus reality is deeply personal. It requires a willingness to reflect, to introspect, and to discern the unique balance between pursuing dreams and maintaining a connection to inner peace and purpose.

To live authentically, one must align their external pursuits with their internal truth. This balance creates a holistic and meaningful existence, where both the pursuit of dreams and the cultivation of inner fulfillment coexist harmoniously.

Clarity and Purpose in Manifestation

To achieve success in manifesting your desires, **clarity and conviction are essential.** The thoughts you impress upon the mental universe must be clear and powerful to leave a meaningful imprint. Vague or inconsistent intentions dissipate like mist, leaving frustration and disappointment in their wake. Life responds to the strength of your focus and the precision of your vision.

Often, the illusion that keeps us from fulfilling our purpose stems from the distractions of daily life. These distractions prevent us from looking inward and uncovering our authentic aspirations.

The true illusion lies in not fulfilling your purpose or living out your dreams, leaving life feeling fragmented and incomplete.

Awareness Shapes Reality

Our level of awareness determines how we interpret life and its events. **Life reveals only what we are capable of understanding.** Just as a painter cannot appreciate the intricacies of a masterpiece without first cultivating their skill, so too do we need to cultivate our awareness to perceive the deeper truths of existence.

Life itself is often likened to a journey, filled with unpredictable twists and turns. Triumphs and defeats are inevitable, but they are not the measure of success. Instead, **the true measure lies in our ability to rise every time we fall.** This resilience, this courage to continue forward, is what shapes a fulfilling life.

Success is not the final destination, nor is failure a dead end. Both are temporary, fleeting moments that shape us but do not define us. **What truly matters is the ability to persevere, to love what we do, and to find meaning even in the most challenging circumstances.**

The Wisdom of Continuance

In the grand scheme of existence, there is one universal truth: **life goes on.** This simple yet profound realization reminds us that no matter the circumstances—whether triumphant or challenging—we are part of an ongoing journey. Each moment is an opportunity to learn, to grow, and to align more closely with our purpose.

By embracing this truth, we transcend the illusions of attachment and disconnection, stepping into a reality where we create meaning through our choices, our thoughts, and our unwavering determination to live authentically. Life is not about escaping illusion entirely but rather about navigating it with awareness, purpose, and grace. **In this dance between illusion and reality, we find the courage to move forward, to rise, and to embrace the truth that, indeed, life goes on.**

Time: The Key to Causality

Deepening your awareness of the true nature of existence unveils the knowledge of **causality**, empowering you to intentionally generate specific causes and influence their subsequent effects. On this earthly plane, **time** serves as a critical mechanism for discerning the relationship between cause and effect. Without the passage of time, the sequential unfolding of events would remain imperceptible, obscuring the intricate interplay between our actions and their outcomes.

Time acts as a **medium of perception**, allowing the observer to recognize and understand how intentions and choices ripple outward, shaping reality. It reveals the interconnectedness of events, granting us the ability to observe patterns and learn from the consequences of our actions.

This temporal framework provides the necessary distance to identify causes, recognize effects, and refine our decisions in alignment with universal principles.

Transcending Time and the Causal Plane

While most of us remain anchored in time, there have been rare individuals who have transcended its influence. These exceptional beings dwell on the **causal plane**, existing beyond the temporal limitations that govern ordinary existence. Through their heightened state of consciousness, they have surpassed the sequential flow of time and grasped a profound understanding of **divine magnetism** —the cosmic force that orchestrates creation and manifestation.

Divine magnetism is not merely an abstract concept but a practical mastery of the universal laws that govern existence. It embodies a conscious alignment with the energetic forces that shape reality. These enlightened beings, free from the constraints of time, perceive causes and effects as simultaneous, effortlessly harmonizing their intentions with the universal rhythms. By embodying this awareness, they wield the ability to manifest with precision, attracting outcomes that resonate with their higher purpose.

Harnessing Causality and Time

For those of us navigating the temporal realm, time remains a powerful teacher and ally. By expanding your awareness and deepening your understanding of causality, you unlock the potential to consciously shape your reality. This requires a deliberate focus on generating **causes rooted in universal alignment**—thoughts, intentions, and actions that resonate with the laws of creation.

Recognizing the connection between cause, effect, and the passage of time offers a profound insight into the workings of the universe. It empowers you to consciously create your reality, aligning your actions with your aspirations. Time becomes not a limitation but a tool—a canvas upon which you paint your destiny, one intentional stroke at a time.

Time as a Mirror of Awareness

Time reflects your level of awareness. It reveals not only the consequences of your past actions but also the opportunities for growth and realignment in the present moment. The more attuned you become to the subtleties of causality, the more you can see how your choices ripple outward. With this clarity, you can make conscious decisions that shape a future aligned with your higher purpose.

While time seems to flow in one direction, its essence is deeply connected to the eternal present. By focusing your awareness on the now, you can tap into the timeless wisdom that exists beyond the linear progression of events. The present moment holds the seed of every cause, and by tending to it with care and intentionality, you can shape the trajectory of your life.

Mastering the Forces of Creation

Through deliberate action and mindful alignment, you gain the ability to influence and direct the effects that manifest in your life. This mastery is not about controlling every outcome but rather harmonizing your intentions with the greater rhythms of the universe. As you deepen your understanding of causality, you learn to work in tandem with these forces, **becoming a co-creator of your reality.**

By expanding your awareness of time and causality, you cultivate the ability to align with **divine magnetism harmonizing** your intentions with the creative forces of the cosmos. This alignment empowers you to manifest with clarity, purpose, and precision, transforming your life into an intentional expression of universal principles.

In this way, time is not merely a measure of moments but a profound tool for understanding and shaping existence. It is through the awareness of time's role in causality that we step into our creative power, becoming deliberate architects of our reality and embracing the infinite potential of the universe.

Fifth Codex

Live as Light

It is evident that the intelligence of a spiritualized individual surpasses that of an evil person. This distinction arises from the profound influence of divine love, which blossoms within the human heart and eradicates ignorance. When divine love permeates the heart, it acts as a transformative force, dissolving the darkness of ignorance and replacing it with the radiant clarity of higher understanding. As one transcends the confines of this earthly realm, they liberate themselves from the clutches of darkness and transition into the realm of luminosity and enlightenment.

The Limits of Human Perception

As humans, we are inherently limited in our ability to perceive and interpret the vastness of existence. We can only perceive a narrow portion of the electromagnetic spectrum, known as visible light, leaving countless dimensions and realities hidden from our awareness. These unseen realities may operate at frequencies, vibrations, or dimensions beyond our current level of understanding. Because our perception is shaped by our sensory and cognitive limitations, each individual experiences and interprets reality uniquely. This is why it is vital to maintain an open mind, to entertain the possibility that what we perceive is but a fragment of a much larger, multidimensional truth.

The Veil of Ignorance and Its Consequences

Ignorance, the root cause of pain and suffering, obstructs genuine awareness and confines understanding to the realm of the physical. It acts as a veil over the luminous consciousness, preventing one from perceiving the divine essence inherent in all things. Within the universal fabric, light and darkness exhibit an inherent magnetic force, attracting or repelling depending on their alignment with truth. Only when the mind achieves tranquility and the heart attains contentment can individuals focus on their higher pursuits. Without peace, the restless mind seeks transient pleasures, leading only to further distress.

However, with the realization of one's true existence and the nature of reality, ignorance loses its grip. The shroud of darkness begins to dissolve, unveiling the authentic self. This unveiling eliminates impurities from both mind and body, preparing the heart for its necessary purification—an essential step, as ignorance repels spiritual light. As darkness recedes, the mind attains clarity, no longer merely reflecting divine light but absorbing and embodying it. This absorption elevates the individual to the state of Christhood, marking a critical transition to higher realms of luminosity, where they embody the essence of a divine Sun.

Ignorance, however, is often deeply rooted in cultural conditioning, religious dogma, environmental factors, education, and familial upbringing. In these cases, the absence of genuine teachers and true knowledge perpetuates the cycle of ignorance, making the pursuit of enlightenment all the more challenging.

Light as the Manifestation of Divine Vibration

Light, the visible manifestation of vibration, serves as a tangible expression of the divine energy that animates all creation. This energy, distinct from artificial sources, is the life-sustaining force synonymous with the divine essence often referred to as "God."

Although the true nature of God remains beyond intellectual comprehension, it can be realized through direct experience. Thoughts, comprising the subtlest elements of creation, possess varying degrees of potency and are designed to harmonize with specific energetic fields or vibrational frequencies. When aligned with these frequencies, thoughts act as catalysts for action and transformation.

The Transformation of Thought Into Reality

The process begins when thoughts are captured by awareness and absorbed into the conscious mind. Through deliberate concentration and contemplation, their energy is amplified, and their vibrational frequency elevated. Over time, these thoughts form structured patterns governed by the law of rhythm, shaping our perception and reality. When repeated consistently, these thought patterns become ingrained in the fabric of nature. Nature, in turn, responds to these patterns by gathering the necessary elements on the causal plane to manifest them as tangible effects in the material world.

The Power of Awareness in a Responsive Universe

This highlights the importance of self-awareness and intentionality in our mental processes, habits, and patterns. The universe is a magical, responsive field that reflects back to us the vibrations we emit. If we move through life unaware and unconsciously maintain a particular vibrational frequency, nature will solidify that state as a permanent reality. For instance, if one adheres to a daily routine devoid of purpose or ambition, nature will reinforce this cycle, leading to a life consumed by monotony. Dreams, aspirations, and the vitality of the mind may wither away, leaving behind a life unfulfilled.

The Rhythm of Creation and the Nature of Duality

The realization of any plan—whether brilliant or detrimental—relies on the consistent rhythm and energy directed toward its fulfillment. This underscores the dual nature of creation in this realm of duality.

In this plane, nature embodies the manifestation of God, encompassing both higher and lower aspects. Our goal is not to align with the desires of lower nature, which perpetuates separation, but to harmonize with the unifying essence of higher nature. This requires the transformation of our own nature to resonate with the entirety of creation.

Vibrational Frequency and Consciousness

As one moves farther from the ultimate Source, vibrational frequency slows. Electromagnetism, a measurable expression of vibrational states, demonstrates this principle: electricity projects while magnetism draws inward. Magnetism, a higher form of electricity, raises vibrational frequency when aligned with the Source. However, beings existing on the same plane may possess vastly different vibrational rates. This disparity arises through consciousness, which determines whether vibrational rates increase or decrease.

Seeking Truth as a Path to the Source

The pursuit of Truth is synonymous with the pursuit of Source, for Truth is an extension of Source itself. By seeking and living in alignment with Truth, we expand our awareness and access higher forms of knowledge. Truth acts as a gateway to elevated consciousness, where the veils of ignorance dissolve, and the light of understanding illuminates the path forward.

Awareness: The Key to Evolution

The distinction between a child and an adult lies in their differing levels of awareness, much like the difference between a "god" and a "man." A child lacks awareness of the potential consequences of their actions, while an adult understands these risks through experience. Similarly, a god's heightened awareness expands their perception and capabilities far beyond those of a man. In darkness, awareness is limited, but in light, revelations unfold, bringing clarity and understanding.

Knowledge as the Foundation of Transformation

Knowledge serves as a guiding light, steadfast amidst the shifting tides of time. Unlike information, which is fluid and ever-changing, true knowledge remains constant. It is through knowledge that one accesses real power—the power to transform, to transcend, and to awaken. Information, though valuable, is powerless without action. Knowledge, on the other hand, possesses the intrinsic ability to ignite profound shifts in consciousness, awakening the spirit to its limitless potential.

SIXTH CODEX

Concentration

Albert Einstein is famously attributed with the statement, *"Compound interest is the most powerful force in the universe."* While this is often associated with financial matters, the principle of compounding reveals a profound truth about the nature of **concentration.** When we direct focused and consistent attention—our mental "interest"—towards a subject or object, we gain a profound understanding of it, uncovering the hidden layers of knowledge it holds.

By consistently applying our concentrated awareness to reality, we engage in a process that leads to **enlightenment.** Concentration and meditation are the tools that allow us to peel back the superficial layers of perception and access the deeper truths of existence. The power of concentrated thought enables us to harness the full potential of our mind, creating a bridge to universal knowledge.

The Triad of Consciousness

The interplay between your **soul, mind, and brain** forms a triad that is pivotal for personal growth. Concentration serves as the link between these three dimensions of consciousness, creating a seamless flow of energy and understanding.

By nurturing this connection, you can transcend the ordinary limits of perception and gain access to **Cosmic Consciousness.** This elevated state of awareness unveils profound truths about yourself and the universe, leading to transformative growth.

However, modern life often diverts us from this path. The distractions of technology, social media, and the incessant demands of daily life fracture our attention and prevent the sustained focus required for self-discovery. These distractions scatter our energy outward, depleting our inner reserves and diminishing our ability to elevate our consciousness.

The Nature of Attention

You've likely heard the phrase, *"Energy follows attention."* This concept reveals a fundamental truth: your energy flows wherever your focus goes. When your senses are constantly directed outward—scrolling through feeds, reacting to external stimuli—you drain your life force. Conversely, by **withdrawing your senses** and concentrating inward, you can conserve and build the energy needed to elevate your awareness.

Concentration is more than just a mental exercise; it is a **spiritual discipline.** By focusing intently on an object with the intention of gaining knowledge, you engage the higher mind, transcending the limitations of the five senses. This allows your mind to become a receiver of knowledge rather than merely a tool for processing external stimuli.

The Power of Deep Focus

When you concentrate deeply on an object, it begins to shine in your mind's eye, opening a channel of communication between you and the object. Over time, this connection deepens, allowing you to **become one with the object.** Its energy field and vibrational frequency reveal themselves to you, granting insight into its essence. This practice requires discipline and the ability to silence drifting thoughts, redirecting all mental energy toward a singular focus.

Many people spend their lives concentrating on superficial distractions—television, social media, trivial pursuits—that yield no meaningful knowledge. Imagine the revelations that could emerge if you directed that same energy toward exploring your inner light. The hidden truths of existence could become clear.

Short Attention Spans and the Suffering They Bring

Today's society has trained many to have short attention spans. This inability to concentrate is a root cause of suffering, as it prevents individuals from achieving greatness or uncovering absolute truths. Concentration is essential for understanding the **ultimate truth,** often referred to as God, which is inseparable from the concept of truth itself. Through sustained focus on the idea of God, we can gain profound insights into our purpose, our potential, and the path we must walk in this lifetime.

Concentration vs. Artificial Intelligence

The rise of artificial intelligence presents an interesting comparison. While AI can process vast amounts of data and generate outputs based on patterns, it lacks the ability to **know.** True knowledge is not the mere accumulation of information but the intuitive understanding that arises from a connection to the **divine mind.** As children of God, we possess the unique ability to access this intuitive knowledge through concentration and meditation—something artificial intelligence can never replicate.

To engage with the **divine mind,** we must develop supreme mental abilities, beginning with the mastery of concentration. This practice allows a steady flow of intuitive knowledge to enter our awareness, connecting us to the source of all truths.

The Foundation of Knowledge

To truly understand the material and spiritual worlds, we must first grasp the fundamental elements of existence: fire, air, earth, water, and ether. Each of these elements corresponds to specific sensory electricities—hearing, seeing, feeling, smelling, and tasting. These senses operate through unique types of electricity traveling along the nervous system, providing us with the tools to navigate the physical plane.

Just as a scientist discovers profound truths through concentrated study—unveiling the atom, subatomic particles, and even the "God particle"—we too can uncover the spirit behind the material world through concentrated focus on the divine. All things originate from God, are sustained by God, and ultimately return to God. This understanding is only accessible through deep, uninterrupted concentration.

The Platform of Awareness

To break free from illusion and distorted thought forms, we must redirect our attention inward. Attention, often referred to as a form of currency, determines the quality of our reality. Spending this "currency" wisely—on self-knowledge and the pursuit of truth—yields profound rewards. Conversely, squandering it on distractions drains our vitality and limits our potential.

When concentration becomes firm, the mind is permeated by **pure consciousness.** This state allows you to access the infinite storehouse of knowledge that surrounds you at all times. Reality, in its truest sense, is not an object to be grasped but a **subject to be experienced.** By entering pure consciousness, you transcend the limitations of ordinary perception and align yourself with the eternal.

Practical Steps to Develop Concentration

To begin cultivating concentration, choose a specific object of interest and focus your attention on it. Analyze its details and hold its image firmly in your mind. Practice directing your focus until the object becomes the sole shining presence in your mind's eye. Repeat this exercise with various subjects—a loved one's face, a piece of art, or a serene landscape.

This practice strengthens your mental discipline and prepares you to tackle greater spiritual challenges. By mastering concentration, you gain the ability to shape your destiny, uncover profound truths, and align with the divine rhythms that govern creation. Concentration is not merely a skill—it is the key to unlocking the boundless potential within you.

The Art of Observation and Concentration

The art of observation is deeply intertwined with the practice of concentration. To refine this skill, dedicate time each evening to reflect on the moments of your day before you rest. Recollect each event, stepping through them as though replaying a film in your mind. This simple exercise sharpens your awareness and hones your ability to observe life's subtleties, strengthening your mental focus.

Once your concentration has matured through consistent practice, you can begin applying this skill in transformative ways. One such application is the **projection of your will**. By focusing your attention on specific areas of your body, you can direct energy for healing or activation. For instance, concentrating on the ganglionic nerve attached to the back of your heart can stimulate and awaken the heart chakra. With focused attention, you align your intent with the energy flow within your body, initiating a process of renewal and activation.

An Advanced Technique for Deepening Concentration

To further refine your concentration, try this advanced exercise:

1. **Immersion in the Present Moment**
    Place yourself in a space where people pass by—a bustling street, a quiet park, or a shared communal area. Observe the movement of these individuals as they traverse the canvas of life. Choose one person—a fleeting presence among the crowd—and focus your attention entirely on them.

2. **Visualization with Eyes Closed**
    Close your eyes and allow the external world to dissolve. With the eyes of your mind wide open, summon the image of this individual. Visualize their face with clarity, tracing each contour and expression. Observe their posture, the way they carry themselves, and their gestures. Seek to understand them not just as a physical being but as a unique essence within the grand symphony of existence.

3. **Delving Beyond the Surface**
    Let your thoughts engage with their potential story—what might their emotions reveal? What energies do they exude? This exercise allows you to intuitively connect with the essence of another being, deepening your capacity for empathy and observation.

4. **Expanding to Nature**
   Extend this practice beyond human interactions. In nature, observe animals, trees, and other living forms. Connect with their primal beauty, witnessing their existence without judgment. Let their presence guide you to a deeper appreciation of the natural world's wisdom.

Transformation Through Deliberate Practice

Through regular practice, your concentration will flourish like a blossoming flower. With each exercise, you chisel away distractions and refine your focus into a potent tool for perception. Over time, the scattered fragments of your attention will converge into a single, unwavering beam of intent. This laser-like focus pierces the veil of noise and distraction, illuminating the path to clarity and self-mastery.

As your ability to concentrate grows, so too does your control over your inner world. You cease to be adrift in the currents of randomness, becoming the captain of your own destiny. Each deliberate act of focus expands your awareness and unlocks the dormant potential within you. You learn to perceive the richness of existence with newfound clarity, transforming your life into a masterpiece of intentionality.

The Mastery of Concentration

Through the mastery of concentration, you awaken to the limitless possibilities that await your exploration. Every breath becomes purposeful, every thought a brushstroke on the canvas of your reality. As you walk this sacred path of self-discovery, guided by the unwavering light of your focused mind, you transcend the ordinary and step into the extraordinary.

This journey is not merely a practice but a transformation —a sacred dance with your inner power. With concentration as your guide, you align with the deeper rhythms of existence, creating a life imbued with purpose, clarity, and fulfillment. Each step reveals a new facet of your potential, reminding you that within you lies the key to unlocking the vast reservoirs of your inner power.

The Use of Altars

Altars are powerful tools that serve as conduits for gathering and focusing energy. They function as a physical representation of your intention, directing your mental, emotional, and spiritual focus toward a specific energy field, concept, or goal. However, it is essential to understand that the altar itself holds no inherent power; it is you, the practitioner, who imbues it with life and purpose. The altar becomes a sacred space where your energy, thoughts, and intentions converge, amplifying your efforts to manifest your desires.

Infusing the Altar with Intention

When utilizing an altar, the spoken word becomes a vital instrument. Words, when infused with raw energy and clear intention, act as a bridge between the seen and unseen realms. Through the vibration of your voice, you project energy outward, influencing the altar and its components without the need for physical contact. This practice requires a deliberate alignment of your will, thoughts, and emotions.

As you speak, visualize the outcome you desire with vivid clarity. Imagine the sensations, emotions, and experiences that accompany the realization of your goal. Feel the energy building within you and flowing through your words into the altar. This process transforms your spoken words into a powerful channel for manifestation, allowing them to influence physical objects and energetic fields alike.

Channeling Raw Energy Through Words

To fully harness the potential of this practice, cultivate the ability to infuse your words with raw energy. This energy originates from your inner reservoir of focus, intention, and spiritual alignment. When you speak with conviction, your words become carriers of your will, vibrating at a frequency that resonates with your intended target.

For instance, when projecting energy toward a specific object or intention on your altar, visualize a beam of light emanating from your words and enveloping the target. See the light pulsating with the power of your intention, transforming and activating the object or concept. This alignment between your inner power and external focus is the essence of effective altar work.

Trusting the Process

Faith and trust are critical elements in this practice. Once you have spoken your words and infused your intention into the altar, release any doubt or hesitation. Trust that your energy has been received and acknowledged by the recipient or target, whether it is a physical object, an abstract concept, or an energetic field. The altar acts as a catalyst, amplifying your energy and facilitating its transmission to the desired destination.

By embracing this process with sincerity and dedication, your altar becomes a powerful tool for transformation. It reflects your inner alignment and commitment to your goals, empowering you to influence and shape your reality. Through the focused use of altars, you connect with the deeper rhythms of existence, harmonizing your intentions with the universal forces that govern creation.

Seventh Codex

ImageNation

The cornerstone of bringing thought forms into reality lies in the crystalline clarity of your visualization. To manifest effectively, you must cultivate and refine your imaginative faculties, creating vivid mental images in your mind's eye with astonishing detail and resolution. Imagination is among your most potent tools for creation, but it requires discipline to tame the mind's unruly nature and prevent wandering thoughts from detracting from your focus.

The Divine Nature of Self-Image

At the core of existence is the quest to understand the "Self"—the essence of who and what you truly are. This journey of self-discovery leads to self-revelation, where you uncover the divine image embedded within your being. The Creator's image is reflected in all of creation, and you, as a manifestation of that divine consciousness, are an integral part of this universal design.

You are not merely a physical entity but an intricate embodiment of divine creativity, residing within the infinite mind of God. Every aspect of your existence—your thoughts, emotions, and actions—contributes to the grand symphony of divine expression.

By embracing this truth, you align yourself with your higher purpose, allowing your inner light to radiate outward, enriching both your life and the world around you.

The Role of the Self-Image in Physical and Mental Health

Your brain and intellect are profoundly influenced by your self-image. Within the brain stem resides the programmed image of yourself, which allows you to transition between wakefulness and sleep. When you sleep, this self-image is temporarily suspended, enabling rest. Upon awakening, it reactivates, restoring your perception of your physical self. This dynamic highlights the power of your self-image in shaping your physical and mental state.

Psychosomatic illnesses often stem from an inability to visualize oneself in action, leading to psychological paralysis. Your subconscious mind, governed by your self-image, orchestrates all involuntary bodily functions. A positive and vibrant self-image harmonizes with your higher self, sustaining the rhythm of your heartbeat and the seamless operation of your body.

When you hold an immaculate mental image of health and vitality, your body's cells respond in alignment, following the mental blueprint you provide. This profound interplay between thoughts, imagery, and physiology underscores the impact of mental health on your overall existence. Like a sculptor shaping clay, your mental imagery molds both your internal and external realities, influencing your beliefs, actions, and experiences.

The Creative Power of Thought and Imagery

The interplay of your thoughts and mental imagery creates a blueprint for your reality. Positive, empowering thoughts paired with vivid, uplifting images attract harmonious vibrations, cultivating growth and well-being. Conversely, negative and limiting thoughts cast shadows, stifling your potential and drawing discordant energies.

By consciously cultivating thoughts of abundance, love, and joy, and vividly visualizing the life you desire, you mold your inner and outer worlds into harmonious reflections of your aspirations. The profound interconnectedness of your internal and external realities makes them responsive to your thoughts and images, empowering you to create a life of fulfillment and purpose.

Transcending Illusions Through a Clear Self-Image

Without a resolute self-image, you risk becoming an indistinct entity, absorbed into the illusions crafted by external influences. However, by meticulously shaping a sharply defined self-image, you emerge as a compelling force, commanding attention and transcending mediocrity.

Conscious imagination holds the power to transform your personal reality and influence the world. The mastery of your psychological and imaginative faculties opens the gateway to transcendent states of existence. Your self-perception and mental imagery serve as guiding forces, propelling you toward your divine destiny.

The Revelation of the True Self

The journey of self-discovery reveals the perfect image of your true self, hidden within the depths of your spirit. This revelation unleashes latent spiritual substances, igniting a wellspring of inner strength and positive motivation. It propels you toward your birthright—realizing divine qualities such as love, wisdom, abundance, and truth.

Your purpose extends beyond mere worship; it is a journey toward realizing your godhood. You are destined to become a radiant "Sun of God," an embodiment of divine essence. By transcending human limitations and embracing self-knowledge, you align with the Creator's will, unlocking the extraordinary within yourself and contributing to the collective evolution of humanity.

Harnessing Zeal and Mental Focus

Zeal is the cosmic flame that propels you through life's journey. It infuses your being with vitality, empowering you to overcome fears and dismantle obstacles. Zeal, paired with sustained mental focus, activates the electric essence of visualization, allowing you to manifest your desires.

When you fixate on thoughts of abundance and prosperity, you align your mental framework with success. By nurturing a mindset attuned to positivity, you invite the realization of your aspirations. Conversely, dwelling on thoughts of failure perpetuates limitation. In a universe abundant with power and knowledge, embracing thoughts of prosperity is essential to realizing your divine potential.

The Power of Divine Alignment

Your inherent nature is one of prosperity, and any notion of failure stems from misalignment with divine truth. When you align your thoughts and intentions with the Creator's will, you become impervious to external forces, manifesting heavenly realms within the earthly domain.

Through mental focus, you create vivid mental images that shape your reality. Your internal landscape influences your external world, rendering your thoughts a powerful tool for transformation. By embracing a positive self-image, nurturing love and abundance, and cultivating zeal, you unlock the potential to manifest your divine essence and contribute to the collective evolution of humanity.

Aim: Entering Pure Consciousness

The ultimate aim of meditation is to immerse oneself in the boundless realm of pure consciousness, where one becomes acutely aware of all aspects of existence and attunes to the sublime elements of their being. At first glance, this may appear contradictory to the process of imagination, for within the realm of pure consciousness, thoughts and manifestations hold no tangible existence. In this state, one experiences the absence of sensory perception—no sights, sensations, sounds, tastes, or other worldly phenomena. However, it is within this heightened state of awareness, this state of pure consciousness, that profound flashes of imagery arise, unveiling deeper layers of understanding.

It is here that prophecies may be unveiled, and symbolism, which serves as divine communication, is imparted. While the goal may be to attain pure consciousness, it is important to recognize that the Creator does not desire us to remain as immobilized beings in that state. Rather, when one reaches the platform of pure consciousness with a receptive heart and mind, they are bestowed with the most extraordinary imagery.

The Role of Self-Image

Reflecting upon our childhood, we may recall instances when a teacher inquired about our aspirations for the future, asking where we envisioned ourselves as we grew older. Similarly, when individuals gauge our perception of personal success, they often inquire about our envisioned trajectory in the next five to ten years. These introspective inquiries highlight the profound significance of self-image —the visualized projection of our potential and desired achievements. Indeed, our self-image holds immense importance in shaping the trajectory of our existence and ultimately contributing to our success.

It is crucial to dedicate a significant portion of your energy and cognitive focus towards uncovering the true essence of your self-image. Simultaneously, it is essential to comprehend the intricacies and nuances of the images that permeate your surroundings, collectively known as creation. Remember, the universe is fundamentally a mental construct, implying that at one point in time, the manifestation of the observable world as we know it may not have existed in the physical realm. In the process of creating something from what appears to be "nothing," the

Creator initially brought forth this manifestation as a mental image. Whatever the Creator envisions materializes, whatever the Creator proclaims becomes reality, and whatever emanates from the Creator assumes existence. Remarkably, you possess this same inherent power, albeit on a smaller scale. It is through the conscious utilization of this power that your life is either shaped or shattered, your reality constructed or dismantled.

Dissolving Into Universal Consciousness

Through the transformative practice of meditation, an individual can enter the realm of pure consciousness, where the confines of the physical body dissolve into the boundless expanse of being. Within this profound state, a remarkable sense of expansiveness unfolds, enabling the individual to perceive themselves as existing ubiquitously, transcending the limitations of time and space. In this heightened state of awareness, conventional notions of reality and separateness give way to a profound understanding of interconnectedness, where the individual becomes a vessel for the universal consciousness that permeates all existence.

The Inner Light Revealed

As you close your eyes during meditation, you consciously disengage from the external visual stimuli, initially encountering a state of darkness. However, as you delve deeper and consciously unravel the intricate web of thoughts that form the veil concealing your inner radiance, a remarkable phenomenon occurs.

The inner realm reveals itself, illuminating your consciousness with its inherent light, and the profound geometric patterns that embody the essence of the Divine become apparent.

The Geometric Symphony of Creation

Creation, in its essence, is the magnificent process of God geometricized. The fundamental building blocks of creation are light waves that carry within them the power to organize and shape atoms into various forms. It is through the interplay of these light waves, vibrating in harmony with the divine blueprint, that the intricate imagery of life unfolds. The divine intelligence encoded within the fabric of creation orchestrates the dance of particles, guiding them to coalesce and form the diverse manifestations we perceive in the physical realm.

The interweaving of light, geometry, and energy provides the foundation upon which this vast creation is intricately woven, revealing the remarkable interconnectedness and inherent order that permeates all aspects of existence. It is through the harmonious interplay of light and geometry that the symphony of creation unfolds, showcasing the boundless creativity and infinite wisdom of the Divine.

The Sacred Geometry of Divine Thought

Every image is an expression of divine geometry, as the energetic vibrations of God's thoughts permeate the universe at an astonishing velocity, manifesting perceptible byproducts both energetically and physically in the form of sacred shapes. Examples of these sacred geometrical forms include the Flower of Life, the Metatron's Cube, and the Star Tetrahedron, among others. These intricate and profound geometric patterns serve as conduits for divine energy and knowledge, offering glimpses into the profound interconnectedness and harmonious organization of the cosmos.

Through meditation and heightened awareness, one gains access to these sacred patterns, allowing for a deeper understanding of the divine structure of existence. By aligning with these universal truths, we become co-creators in the ongoing symphony of life, resonating with the infinite wisdom of the Creator.

Imagery Technique: Becoming the Master Architect

Envision yourself as the master architect, meticulously designing a grand edifice. With unwavering attention to detail, embark upon the construction process, infusing vitality into the blueprint and transmuting it into a living picture. Focus your mind to an unparalleled state of concentration, fixating unwaveringly on the singular idea or object you aspire to manifest. Engage with it as though it exists tangibly in the present moment. Maintain a resolute hold on this object or idea within your mind's eye, cultivating a profound level of clarity and intricacy. Sustain this mental image for a minimum of two minutes, harnessing the power of your mental faculties. The magnitude of transformation you achieve is directly proportional to the magnitude of energy you invest.

Through wholehearted practice, you shall begin the seemingly magical orchestration of all requisite elements converging to manifest your envisioned reality. The universe, ever responsive, swiftly aligns with the intensity of your energetic input.

Clearing Obstacles to Infinite Possibilities

Understand that this process entails more than mere contemplation; it demands enthusiastic action to clear obstacles and unlock the door of infinite possibilities across all conceivable avenues. This unrestricted passage facilitates the graceful convergence of necessary components toward your energetic field. Once these elemental forces entwine harmoniously with the fabric of your mind, their arrival becomes discernible if you steadfastly maintain a psychological assumption of their inevitable actualization. Remain prepared to seize every opportunity that presents itself, undeterred by any momentary setbacks. Cultivate unwavering confidence and infuse your idea with boundless love, for it is through this passion that your envisioned reality is assuredly brought into existence.

Distinguishing Random Thinking from Focused Imagery

The distinction between random thinking and engaging in imagery lies in the level of focus, intention, and control over the mind's activities. Random thinking occurs when the mind passively absorbs various stimuli from the environment—such as a song you heard at the gas station or a conversation from a recent podcast—without conscious direction. These thoughts emerge spontaneously as the subconscious mind replays stored information, constantly processing and retrieving data.

In contrast, actively engaging in imagery harnesses the power of concentration and willpower. By directing your thoughts toward a specific goal or purpose, you exercise control over your mind's activities. Instead of drifting aimlessly, you become anchored to a particular image, preventing your thoughts from scattering in a chaotic manner.

Taming the Mind Through Imagination

Building your imagination serves as a method to tame your mind and bring it under your command. The goal is not to forcefully shut down the mind but rather to develop mastery over it. Through regular meditation, you can enhance your awareness of your thoughts and gain greater control over them. This practice enables you to train your mind to disregard distractions and maintain unwavering focus on your objectives. Negative thought patterns can be identified and replaced with positive, constructive thoughts, allowing you to take charge of your mind as a potent instrument for realizing your goals and leading a more rewarding existence.

Cultivating Inner Peace and Mindfulness

By cultivating a disciplined mind, you create the conditions for inner peace and harmony. Letting go of negative emotions and promoting a positive, joyful outlook on life generates a profound sense of self-awareness.

Mindfulness practices are essential in taming the mind, enabling you to navigate your thoughts and emotions with intention. As a result, you can lead a more fulfilling and purposeful life. Through focused imagery and disciplined practice, you become the master of your mental realm, aligning yourself with the infinite potential within.

Prayer: The Art of Creative Visualization

A profound approach to prayer involves the deliberate and conscious construction of vivid imagery within the mind's eye, paired with the unwavering affirmation that this imagery will manifest into reality. By projecting your will and intentions into the vast ethers, you actively engage with the fundamental elements of creation. This sacred process connects you to the Divine, reminding you that everything, including yourself, is inherently crafted in the image and likeness of the Creator.

The Power of Visualization in Prayer

At the heart of prayer lies the ability to construct vivid mental imagery. When you engage in prayer, imagine the details of what you wish to manifest with astonishing clarity. See the colors, feel the textures, hear the sounds, and immerse yourself in the essence of the desired outcome. Your mind becomes a canvas, and your thoughts are the brushstrokes that paint the vision of your aspirations.

This process is more than a passive visualization; it is an intentional projection of your will into the vast ethers—the unseen fabric that connects all elements of creation. In this space, your thoughts resonate as vibrational frequencies, interacting with the universal field and initiating the alignment of circumstances, people, and opportunities to bring your vision into reality.

Aligning with the Divine Image

Recognize that you are crafted in the image and likeness of the Divine. This acknowledgment is not a mere philosophical concept but a profound truth that underscores your inherent creative power. By embracing this truth, you align your consciousness with the universal intelligence that governs all existence.

Your prayers, when infused with this awareness, transcend the limitations of the physical plane. They become acts of divine co-creation, harmonizing your desires with the infinite potential of the cosmos. In this state, you are not separate from the Creator but an active participant in the unfolding of creation itself.

The Practice of Prayerful Visualization

- **Enter a State of Calm**: Begin your prayer by quieting the mind. Enter a state of stillness where distractions fade, and your awareness becomes fully present.
- **Construct Your Vision**: Envision what you desire to manifest with precision and detail. Imagine the end result as if it already exists. Feel the joy, peace, or abundance that accompanies its realization.
- **Embrace Possibilities**: In your visualization, explore unconventional and innovative paths that could lead to the fulfillment of your prayer. Allow the mental plane to transcend the boundaries of the physical world, opening doors to limitless possibilities.
- **Infuse with Emotion**: The power of your prayer lies not only in the clarity of your vision but also in the strength of your emotions. Feel gratitude as if your desire has already been granted. Let this emotion saturate your entire being.
- **Project Your Intention**: With your vision firmly in place, project it into the ethers. Imagine your thought-form taking shape, radiating energy that ripples across the universe. Trust that the forces of creation are aligning to bring your vision to fruition.
- **Release and Act**: Surrender your prayer to the universe with faith and certainty. Align your actions with the insights received during your visualization, creating harmony between intention and effort.

Tapping into the Infinite Potential

Through the practice of prayerful visualization, you harmonize your consciousness with the boundless creative forces of the universe. In the mental plane, all things are possible, and by tapping into this potential, you transcend conventional boundaries. Your prayers become a bridge between the seen and unseen, a channel through which divine energy flows to manifest your highest aspirations.

Living in the Spirit of Prayer

Prayer is not confined to specific moments but can become a continuous state of being. As you move through life, carry the awareness that your thoughts, words, and actions are constant expressions of prayer. By maintaining a mindset of gratitude, love, and creative possibility, you align yourself with the higher realms of consciousness and actively participate in the co-creation of a reality that reflects your divine essence.

In this way, prayer becomes more than a ritual; it transforms into a way of life—a profound connection to the infinite intelligence that guides, sustains, and empowers all of creation. Through prayer, you embody the truth that you are both the created and the creator, shaping your reality with the power of imagination, intention, and divine alignment.

Fear: The Energy That Constricts and Distorts

Fear causes you to perceive the world around you as a perpetual threat, leading to a distorted sense of extreme self-preservation. This distorted perspective can push you into isolation, where avoidance becomes your primary coping mechanism. When left unchecked, fear constricts both the physical body and the astral body—where the chakra system resides. This constriction creates perpetual contradictions within your field of awareness. As the energetic field vibrates and spins out of alignment, improper thought forms emerge, leading to the habitual projection of negative emotions and a tendency toward low-vibratory activities. A weakened connection to the Creator leaves you feeling unfulfilled, vulnerable, and increasingly reliant on unhealthy attachments as a remedy for the dissociation from your divine source.

Fear and worry serve as internal signals indicating that your thought patterns require purification. Most fears stem from learned behaviors: social programming, a lack of knowledge, distorted self-images, misunderstanding, and even epigenetic memories encoded in your DNA. Among all fears, the fear of death and the unknown leaves the most profound impression on the mental body. But why fear death? The fragility of the physical form means that it is merely a vessel, destined to one day return to its source. Fearing what is inevitable only constricts the flow of life, which is designed to evolve beyond the physical.

Cleansing the Mind of Fear

To overcome fear, begin by confronting it in a meditative state. Sit with your greatest fears, analyzing them without emotional interference. Simply observe them as they are—raw and unembellished. Then, envision the counter-emotion to each fear: courage. Picture yourself embodying courage and taking control of that fear, turning its energy into strength. Affirm your fearlessness and resolve during this meditation. When you arise from this practice, carry with you the strength cultivated within. Repeat this process until fear has no dominion over you.

Fear, worry, and anxiety impose physical consequences as well. These imbalances constrict the body's blood vessels, hindering homeostasis and reducing the overall vitality of the physical and energetic systems. The astral body—your subtle energetic counterpart—draws closer to the physical body under the weight of harmful frequencies from Wi-Fi, cell towers, and other environmental stressors. As it constricts, your astral body becomes vulnerable, and your physical health suffers as a result. This constriction diminishes vitality, impairs mental faculties, and gives rise to chaotic thought patterns, further restricting liberation and clarity.

When your astral body is compromised, you are cut off from higher-frequency vibrations that elevate consciousness. Adversaries exploit this constriction by inundating you with fear, confusion, and environmental pollutants that further congest your system. As a result, your auric field, which should extend for miles, contracts to mere inches around your body. This reduction makes it difficult for beings of higher planes to see or assist you.

Like a plant deprived of water, your system begins to wither without the sustenance of incoming intelligence and divine light.

Constriction equals restriction. It obstructs the flow of divine energy in your life. Only by aligning your actions and thoughts with your divine purpose can you release this constriction and manifest a reality aligned with your higher self.

The Astral Body and Emotional Signatures

The astral body can be likened to the event horizon of a black hole—a space where emotional experiences are stored as energetic imprints. Just as matter disintegrates at a black hole's edge, emotional memories are retained at the surface of the astral body. These imprints persist beyond physical death, carried across incarnations until they are processed and integrated. Each lifetime offers an opportunity to delve into this repository of experiences, extracting lessons and growth. This continual process leads to profound evolution on a soul level, unlocking wisdom that propels you toward higher states of being.

Facing Pain and Fear: Tools for Purification

Pain and fear, while uncomfortable, act as purifiers for the mind. When you encounter these challenges, they signal impurities that require cleansing. Accept these experiences rather than resisting them. By moving through them with courage, you emerge stronger and more aligned with your higher self. Through this process, you unlock hidden potentials that fear once obscured, revealing profound abilities within you.

As your mind frees itself from impurities, it transcends sensory limitations, granting access to latent powers. The purification of the mind not only liberates you from fear but also sharpens your vision of the divine. This clarity enables you to create a life guided by higher wisdom.

The Role of Vision and Imagination in Overcoming Fear

Visualization and imagination are tools of great power, but they can be double-edged swords. When the mind fixates on false images, it creates an internal breeding ground for fears. Imagine mistaking a garden hose for a snake in the dark. The false image triggers fear, but the illumination of light dissolves it instantly. Similarly, becoming conscious of your thoughts and dismantling false mental constructs dissolves fear at its roots.

Vision extends far beyond the physical eyes. It is a faculty of the spirit, an energy current of one of the five electricities that govern perception. In dreams, where physical eyes play no role, you still "see" vividly. This demonstrates that vision is not bound by physical constraints but is instead an innate quality of the mind. By mastering this current, you can see through and beyond physical reality, even perceiving across dimensions or tapping into another's perspective.

Freedom Through Mastery of Fear

Freedom lies in mastering fear rather than succumbing to it. By embracing the challenges fear presents, you transform its energy into growth. This alchemical process strengthens your astral and physical bodies while harmonizing them with divine frequencies. As you overcome fear and embrace your higher potential, your auric field expands, your vibrational frequency rises, and your consciousness becomes a beacon of light that aligns you with the Creator's will. Fear no longer serves as an obstacle but as a tool for self-realization and spiritual transcendence.

Eighth codex

Manifestation

Becoming a proficient visualizer requires dedicated practice, unwavering commitment, and steadfast determination. Mastering the art of visualization is the initial step towards becoming an adept manifestor, as your ability to manifest your desires relies heavily on your visualization skills.

Nourishment for Manifestation

To support your mental health and optimize the functioning of your physical brain, it is crucial to nourish yourself with highly nutritious foods, herbs, and supplements that provide essential nutrients for brain health. This holistic approach acknowledges the interconnectedness of the mind and body, recognizing the importance of maintaining a balanced and nourished system. Additionally, cultivating a sense of inner peace and maintaining control over your mind is vital. Striving for equilibrium in all aspects of your life contributes to overall well-being and enhances your manifestation abilities. This includes cultivating healthy sexual habits, understanding that balance and moderation are fundamental principles in achieving harmonious outcomes.

The Power of Consistent Visualization

It is important to remember that the power of manifestation is not instantaneous. Merely practicing visualization once or a few times does not guarantee immediate results. It takes time and consistent effort to train your mind to vividly and intricately visualize your desires during meditation. However, with persistence and dedication, you will eventually reach a state where your visualizations become as clear as if your eyes were open in the physical realm. At that juncture, you will have the ability to harness the primordial resources necessary to materialize your envisioned reality.

Belief Shapes Reality

Indeed, the power of belief plays a crucial role in the manifestation process. It is not enough to simply desire something; you must genuinely believe that you are capable of attaining your desires. Your beliefs shape your reality, and if you hold contradictory beliefs, such as desiring abundance while simultaneously believing in scarcity or poverty, it creates a dissonance that hinders the manifestation of your desires.

Poverty as an Illusion

Poverty is an illusion, a construct of distorted thinking that stems from a limited understanding of the infinite abundance present in creation. True spiritual prosperity encompasses both material and mental well-being and does not exclude any aspect of life. It is important to recognize that renunciation, as practiced by spiritual figures throughout history, was a demonstration of their spiritual power rather than a necessity. They possessed the ability to manifest anything they desired, as they understood the abundance of the universe.

Embracing Spiritual Prosperity

It is crucial not to fall into the trap of justifying poverty or lack with spirituality. Such a perspective can be detrimental to your mental health and overall well-being. Embracing spiritual prosperity means aligning your beliefs with the abundance of the universe, dismantling limiting beliefs, and cultivating a mindset of abundance in all areas of life. This shift in perspective allows you to tap into the infinite possibilities that exist and manifest the life of abundance and fulfillment that you desire.

True Manifestation Beyond Constructs

When I speak of manifesting desires, I am not merely referring to success within the constructs of the financial matrix or societal illusions created by an elite class of rulers. True manifestation occurs when an individual taps into their oneness with the divine Creator and creates profound changes within the universe and the world. This may include the removal of ignorance, healing abilities, the creation of a divine environment on the planet, and other spiritually impactful outcomes. The focus is on elevating consciousness and creating transformational change on a profound level, rather than materialistic gain within man-made constructs.

Perception and Reality

The nature of your reality is intricately tied to your perception. Therefore, it becomes paramount to cultivate a pristine and unobstructed mind, receptive to the divine frequencies that facilitate the generation of accurate thought patterns—ones guided by the divine essence. It is crucial to avoid distorted thinking and instead harness the power of focused will, firmly believing in your ability to manifest the intentions you have formulated within the depths of your mind's eye.

Aligning Desires and Beliefs

It is important to acknowledge that the mere desire for wealth does not automatically lead to its manifestation, especially if one harbors beliefs that equate money with malevolence or considers it to be the root of all evil. Money, in itself, possesses neither life nor power, as it lacks the essence of a living entity. It is rather the insatiable craving for wealth that can provoke corrupt thoughts and actions in individuals. Bridging the gap between your desires and beliefs is essential to tap into the potency of willpower, enabling you to truly believe in your capacity to attain what you seek.

The Magnetic Force of Love

Love, as a magnetic force, draws toward you that which aligns with your desires, exemplifying the power of the law of attraction. This universal law operates by attracting what you hold as a corresponding mental image. To activate this process, you must first develop a vivid mental representation of your desires.

Without a mental equivalent, the physical manifestation remains elusive. For instance, if your desire is to possess a house, you must immerse yourself mentally in its intricacies, envisioning every detail—imbibe its scents, resonate with its sounds, and immerse yourself in the tangible sensations it evokes.

Shifting Focus from Lack

In order to free yourself from contradictory thought patterns, it is crucial to shift your focus away from dwelling on your current state of lack, especially if you desire wealth. The mind attracts what it consistently dwells upon, and hence, it is essential to polarize your thoughts toward the manifestation of your desires and maintain unwavering determination. Consciously affirm your desires and project your intentions out into the vastness of the universe, creating powerful ripples in the fabric of space-time that draw precisely what you seek toward you.

The Resonance of Thought Forms

To effectively manifest your desires, it is necessary to generate an energetic field that aligns with what you intend to manifest. By creating thought forms infused with the specific vibrations of your desired outcome, you establish a resonance that attracts corresponding energies into your reality. Everything you consciously and subconsciously cognize becomes an energy field that emanates from you.

Energy Fields and External Reflections

The frequencies we emit entangle with similar frequencies in our environment, resulting in encounters with people, places, and things that mirror our internal emotional and mental states. Our external situations and circumstances serve as reflections of the energies we carry within ourselves. By understanding this dynamic, we gain insight into the profound influence our internal space holds over our external experiences.

Elementals and the Dance of Creation

Through the power of concentration and focused cognition, you create an energy vortex around the thoughts you hold. This vortex generates a rhythmic pattern, forming an energetic field that interacts with the subtle forces known as "elementals." These elementals act as messengers, traversing the vast expanse of the ether, spanning across worlds and universes. Their purpose is to attract to you the equivalent manifestations of the specific energy vibration that was initially set in motion by your original intention.

The Orchestration of Manifestation

As these elementals journey through the ethers, they work in harmony with the cosmic laws, drawing forth people, places, things, and situations that align with the vibrational essence you have infused into your energy field.

Every encounter and experience that comes into your reality is intricately linked to this process. The synchronized dance between your energy field and the universal energies guides the flow of manifestations, bringing forth the desired forms designed by the original intention that birthed them. Your conscious participation in shaping this energetic dance allows you to co-create your reality and attract the experiences that align with your intentions.

Ninth codex

The Active Mind vs. The Passive Mind

The eternal dance of existence revolves around the primordial essence known as Source, the origin from which all manifestations arise. Source represents the infinite wellspring of creation, the pure and undefiled essence that remains untouched by limitation. At the first degree of separation from this ultimate unity lies the genesis of all elements that compose the fabric of existence—an ethereal realm often described as "chaos." Here, Source acts as the divine conductor, orchestrating harmony from the seemingly discordant threads of creation's ingredients, weaving them into a purposeful design according to its divine will.

This boundless expanse, often referred to as the Universal Mind, is the foundation of all existence. It serves as the matrix in which every conceivable manifestation is intricately woven, forming a unified whole that transcends the individual and merges into the collective field of being. To understand Source is to recognize that all things arise from and return to this infinite intelligence.

Alignment with Source: The Key to Unlimited Power

When one's consciousness becomes singularly focused on Source—steady, unwavering, and free from distraction—a profound transformation occurs. This alignment is not merely a mental exercise but a spiritual attunement that elevates one's being to resonate with the ultimate power of creation. In this communion, the individual transcends the fragmented self and merges into the realm of pure consciousness, the very domain where all abilities, powers, and divine faculties find their origin.

In this state, manifestation is no longer an act of effort or willful striving but a natural and effortless unfolding. Desires aligned with divine will flow seamlessly into existence, not because of human force but because they are carried by the currents of divine harmony. This is the essence of true power—an unshakable connection to the Source that enables the individual to co-create with the boundless intelligence that sustains all existence.

To be connected to Source is to be inundated with unimaginable power. This connection activates and enhances every aspect of the individual—mental faculties sharpen to a superlative degree, chakras spin with unparalleled clarity and vitality, and spiritual abilities blossom into their fullest potential. True power arises not from external tools or techniques but from this intimate alignment with Source, the ultimate reservoir of all abilities.

The Nameless: The Infinite Creator Beyond Perception

The Nameless, often referred to as the Unknowable One, stands as the supreme subject underlying all existence. This essence is beyond objectivity, transcending the finite constructs of the human mind. While objects belong to creation, the Subject is the Creator itself—a presence that cannot be grasped through thought, language, or sensory experience. It is not an object to be understood but a divine truth to be experienced.

Through deep contemplation and meditation on pure consciousness, the mind is elevated beyond its usual confines. In this elevation, the individual moves closer to the infinite Subject, experiencing a profound connection with the Source. This connection is not intellectual but experiential, revealing the divine essence within and without.

The Foundation of Consciousness: The Inner Spark

At the core of every being lies the Foundation of Consciousness, an inner spark that is the same in all things. This spark is the eternal flame of Source within creation, a permanence that transcends time, space, and form. It serves as the wellspring of all transformations, the inexhaustible reservoir from which all life and potential flow.

When this spark is consciously activated through alignment with Source, the individual becomes a channel for divine power. Every action, thought, and intention becomes a reflection of divine will, radiating outward to shape reality. In this state, the barriers of limitation dissolve, revealing the interconnectedness of all things and the boundless possibilities that arise from this unity.

Psychic and Spiritual Abilities: Expressions of Connection

The ultimate psychic and spiritual abilities—whether the ability to heal, manifest, or perceive beyond the physical—stem from this profound connection to Source. When fully aligned, the individual becomes a vessel through which the infinite intelligence and power of the Creator flow. Every act of manifestation, every miraculous event, and every heightened faculty of perception is a byproduct of this alignment.

These abilities are not external tricks or isolated phenomena but the natural expression of divine connection. To strengthen this connection is to unlock the full spectrum of human and spiritual potential. The closer one moves to Source, the more the boundaries of the physical world dissolve, and the innate powers of the spirit emerge.

When the mind is free of distortion, the chakras are clear, and the energetic pathways are open, the individual resonates fully with Source. In this state, even the most extraordinary feats—manifesting desires, transcending time and space, perceiving unseen realms—become second nature. Source is the key, and alignment is the doorway.

Becoming One with Source

To align with Source is to embrace your highest potential. It is to reconnect with the infinite wellspring of power and wisdom that resides within and flows through all things. In this alignment, all abilities become possible, and the limitations of the material world fall away. The eternal dance of existence becomes a harmonious symphony, and the individual, once fragmented, becomes whole—a true co-creator with the divine.

This is the essence of spiritual mastery: to live in constant alignment with Source, drawing upon its infinite power to illuminate the path of existence, manifest the divine will, and transform the world within and around you.

The Spiritualized Atom: A Vessel of Divine Creation

In the spiritual realm, the atom is not merely a fundamental building block of matter but a profound conduit of divine potential, resonating with elevated frequencies that transcend the purely material. Scientifically, the atom is the basic unit of physical reality, yet its metaphysical significance lies in its capacity to bridge the physical and the spiritual. An "elevated frequency" signifies the atom's vibration aligned with higher planes of existence, where it becomes a vessel for divine intelligence and creative energy, embodying the unity of all things.

The sacred syllable "OM," often regarded as the primordial sound of creation, represents the essence of this unity. It symbolizes the convergence of time, space, and the atomic structure, encapsulating the harmony between the tangible and intangible aspects of existence. This vibrational resonance connects the atom's subtle energy with the universal fabric, weaving together the physical and the eternal.

These elements—*OM*, sound, time, space, and the atom—though distinct in our perception, are unified expressions within divine creation. The atom, as a microcosm of this unity, acts as a celestial mirror, reflecting the radiance of the Creator and participating in the generation of the cosmos. Just as light reflects off a surface, divine light moves through and animates every atom, imbuing it with creative potential. Recognizing this reveals a profound truth: as collections of atoms, we are living embodiments of divine intention, surfaces upon which the Creator's light shines. This insight calls us to understand our role as active participants in divine creation.

Yet, the atom also carries within it the "residue of obscurity"—metaphysical fragments of darkness that represent the limitations inherent in physical existence. These residues symbolize the challenges that obscure our comprehension of spiritual illumination, reminding us that the journey toward enlightenment requires transcending these barriers to fully embody divine light.

The Dance of Atoms: Physical Interaction and Spiritual Insight

Physical contact, often taken for granted, is not merely a surface-level interaction. It is, in essence, a dance of opposing atomic forces. When two objects or beings come into "contact," their atoms do not actually touch in the way we might imagine. Instead, a repulsive force between their atomic fields generates the sensation of touch. This interplay arises because atoms, governed by physical laws, cannot coexist in the same spatial domain.

Understanding this dynamic opens a metaphysical perspective: touch is more than a physical sensation; it is an energetic exchange, a moment where the boundaries between beings are both affirmed and transcended. It symbolizes the interconnectedness of all existence, even in the seeming separateness of physical forms.

The Five Electricities: Foundational Forces of Creation

Within this cosmic choreography of atoms lies the genesis of five distinct manifestations of electricity—subtle, energetic forces that underpin all of creation. These electric currents are drawn toward a central point by the magnetic force of love, the ultimate unifying energy of the cosmos. Love, as the magnetic force, acts as the binding agent, harmonizing these electricities into a cohesive whole.

These five electricities represent the primal energetic forces that govern the formation and transformation of existence. They are:

1. **Creative Electricity**: The force responsible for bringing new forms into being.
2. **Sustaining Electricity**: The energy that maintains order and balance within creation.
3. **Transformative Electricity**: The force that drives change and evolution, breaking down old forms to make way for the new.
4. **Harmonic Electricity**: The energy that orchestrates the interplay of all forces, ensuring their alignment with divine order.

5. **Illuminating Electricity**: The light-bearing energy that reveals the divine essence within all things.

These forces converge upon the ultimate reality—God, the Source of all existence. In their unity, they generate a magnetic field that embodies divine intelligence and order, shaping the cosmos with precision and purpose. This magnetic field, often described as the "body of intelligence," is the medium through which divine will manifests in creation.

The Atom as a Gateway to Unity

The five electricities emanating from the atom form the causal framework for all existence, acting as the roots of creation and the energetic foundation of the "Sun of God"—the radiant source of life and illumination. These forces permeate every aspect of the universe, orchestrating the intricate dance of existence and revealing the interconnectedness of all things.

To perceive the atom in this way is to recognize it as a microcosm of the divine order. The atom, while seemingly insignificant, holds the blueprint of creation within its structure. Its vibrations, interactions, and energies mirror the larger cosmic patterns, offering a glimpse into the divine intelligence that governs all.

By understanding the spiritualized atom, we gain insight into the seamless interplay between the physical and metaphysical. The atom becomes a bridge between worlds —a tangible reminder that the physical universe is but a reflection of a far greater spiritual reality.

In this light, the journey of enlightenment involves attuning our awareness to the elevated frequencies of the atom and aligning ourselves with the divine energies it channels.

The Five Electricities and Human Senses: The Pathway to Expanded Perception

The five electricities, as foundational forces in creation, find their counterparts within the human body, manifesting as the electric currents that govern our five primary senses: sight, hearing, taste, touch, and smell. These senses are not merely physiological functions but profound energetic gateways through which we interact with the external world. Each sense corresponds to a distinct electric current, traveling along the nervous system, activating specific sensory experiences and shaping our perception of reality.

Unique Frequencies of Sensory Electricities

Each sense operates through its own unique frequency of electricity, tailored to its specific function. These electric currents, traveling along nerves, serve as bridges between the physical and energetic realms:

1. **Sight (Vision):** The electric current responsible for sight is a luminous frequency, finely tuned to process light waves and translate them into visual

images. This electricity flows through the optic nerves, creating a connection between the physical eye and the mind's perception of form and color.

2. **Hearing (Audition):** The electricity of hearing vibrates at an auditory frequency, carrying sound waves along the auditory nerves to the brain. This current allows the human mind to interpret vibrations in the air as meaningful patterns of sound.

3. **Touch (Tactile Perception):** The electricity of touch generates an intricate network of impulses along sensory nerves, detecting variations in pressure, texture, and temperature. This frequency governs the sensation of physical contact, making the intangible forces of the world tangible to human awareness.

4. **Taste (Gustation):** The electricity of taste is a frequency attuned to the chemical interactions within the taste buds, converting the essence of flavors into sensory experiences. This current allows the individual to engage directly with the physical substances of their environment.

5. **Smell (Olfaction):** The electricity of smell vibrates at a frequency capable of interpreting molecular structures as olfactory sensations. This current travels along the olfactory nerves, linking the physical world of aromas to the emotional and intuitive centers of the brain.

Expanding Beyond the Individual: Tapping into Universal Sensory Fields

By understanding the unique frequencies of these electricities, it becomes possible to extend perception beyond the confines of the individual body. This mastery requires attunement to the subtle energetic signatures of the sensory electricities and the ability to harmonize with them through conscious intention and willpower.

Tapping into the Field of Vision

The electricity that governs sight, when attuned to its subtle frequency, holds the potential to perceive beyond one's own physical eyes. By aligning with the luminous frequency of vision, it is conceivable to tap into another's visual field, seeing through their eyes and accessing their perspective across space and time. This process requires the practitioner to synchronize with the target's visual electricity, creating a shared energetic field where their vision becomes accessible.

Accessing the Auditory Field

Similarly, the electricity of hearing can be harnessed to transcend physical distance and perceive sounds originating from another location or being. By attuning to the auditory frequency, one can tap into the soundscapes experienced by others, even across vast expanses of space-time. This ability aligns with the principle that sound, as vibration, carries its energetic signature eternally in the ether.

Bridging the Sensory Gap

The remaining senses—touch, taste, and smell—are equally accessible through mastery of their respective electricities. For example, the tactile frequency allows one to feel sensations experienced by another, while the gustatory and olfactory frequencies open pathways to share in the tastes and aromas encountered by others. These abilities highlight the interconnectedness of all beings and the universal field of sensory experiences.

The Mechanics of Sensory Transcendence

At its core, the process of tapping into another's sensory field relies on the principle of **frequency resonance.** Every sensory electricity emits a unique vibrational pattern, which can be accessed by matching its frequency through focused intention, concentration, and alignment with the universal energy field. Here's how it works:

1. **Frequency Tuning:** The practitioner must enter a heightened state of awareness, meditating on the specific sensory electricity they wish to access. This state allows the mind to transcend the physical body and synchronize with the desired frequency.

2. **Energetic Linking:** Once the frequency is matched, the practitioner establishes an energetic connection to the target individual or location. This connection serves as a conduit for sensory information, enabling the practitioner to perceive as if they were present in the target's field.

3. **Trans-Spatial Awareness:** Because electricities operate on universal principles, they are not bound by physical distance. This allows the practitioner to perceive across vast expanses of space-time, accessing sensory fields in other locations or even moments in time.

Metaphysical Implications and Mastery

The ability to access and manipulate these sensory electricities is not merely a demonstration of skill but a profound reminder of the interconnectedness of all existence. Each sensory electricity serves as a thread in the fabric of universal consciousness, weaving together the experiences of all beings into a unified field of perception.

Mastering this art requires disciplined practice, a clear mind, and an unwavering alignment with divine will. It is through this alignment that the practitioner can transcend the limitations of individual sensory perception and tap into the collective sensory field of creation. This mastery unlocks new dimensions of awareness, allowing one to:

- Perceive the world through another's eyes or ears, developing profound empathy and understanding.
- Expand their own sensory experiences, enriching their connection to the universe.
- Harness the power of sensory electricities for healing, insight, and spiritual growth.

The Infinite Potential of Sensory Electricities

The five sensory electricities, when fully understood and mastered, reveal the limitless potential of human perception. They are not merely physiological functions but divine tools for experiencing and interacting with creation. By transcending the physical boundaries of the senses, we open the door to a reality where perception knows no limits—a reality where we truly become one with the universal field of consciousness.

This knowledge serves as a reminder that we are not isolated beings but interconnected facets of a greater whole. Each sense, powered by its unique electricity, offers a pathway to deeper unity and understanding, calling us to explore the boundless possibilities of perception and the divine energy that sustains it.

Expanding the Five Electricities: The Sensory Pathways

The five electricities that govern human sensory experiences are not only the foundation of our physical interaction with the world but also serve as keys to unlocking profound metaphysical abilities. These electric currents travel along the nerves, each uniquely tailored to generate one of the five senses as discussed: sight, hearing, taste, touch, and smell. The electricity enabling sight, for instance, is distinct from the one that facilitates hearing, operating at a unique frequency and vibration.

The human sensory experience is, therefore, an intricate symphony of specialized electricities. Each current resonates with a particular vibrational frequency, making it possible for one to see light, hear sound, feel textures, taste flavors, or detect scents. By mastering the understanding and manipulation of these electric currents, one could transcend the boundaries of their individual sensory perceptions.

The Phenomenon: Tapping into Another's Electric Current

A man once demonstrated an extraordinary ability to see through the eyes of anyone who entered his space while he was asleep. When someone walked into his room, he could describe, with uncanny accuracy, what that person was seeing—even though his physical eyes were closed. This astonishing phenomenon suggests that he had mastered the art of tuning into another person's electrical current of sight, effectively aligning his consciousness with their sensory field.

This ability highlights the profound potential of human perception when the barriers of individuality are transcended. The man's unique connection to his environment and those within it offers a glimpse into how the five electricities can operate beyond the confines of the physical body.

Theoretical Pathway to Accessing Another's Sensory Circuitry

This phenomenon, though rare, suggests that certain conditions and practices could enable one to tap into another person's sensory current. Below is an exploration of how this might theoretically be achieved:

1. Expanding and Anchoring the Auric Field

The man's ability likely stemmed from a highly developed auric field that extended beyond his physical body and merged with the energetic fields of others entering his space. By anchoring his energy deeply within the room, his auric field became a dynamic network, sensitive to all energetic vibrations within that environment.

- **Practice:** Focus on auric expansion meditations. Visualize your energy filling your space, creating an interconnected web that detects subtle changes when others enter.

2. Resonance and Frequency Matching

Tapping into another's sensory current involves achieving resonance with their sensory electricities. For sight, this would mean aligning with the unique frequency of their visual circuitry.

- **Practice:** Meditate on the vibrational essence of sight. Visualize aligning your consciousness with the visual frequency of another person, imagining yourself "seeing through their eyes."

3. Spatial Sensory Awareness

The ability may be heightened in specific spaces, such as the man's room, where his energetic field had established dominance. This anchoring created a localized resonance, making it easier to interface with the sensory currents of others.

- **Practice:** Establish an energetic presence in a space by repeatedly grounding and expanding your energy there. Develop a habit of sensing shifts in the field when others enter.

4. The Role of Altered States

The fact that the man achieved this while asleep suggests that altered states of consciousness—such as deep meditation, REM sleep, or trance—lower the mental barriers that typically separate individual sensory fields. These states allow the subconscious to expand and interact with external energies more freely.

- **Practice:** Experiment with lucid dreaming and intention-setting before sleep. Affirm your desire to perceive the sensory currents of others who enter your field.

Metaphysical Implications

The implications of mastering the five electricities extend far beyond individual perception. If one could reliably access another's sensory field, this ability could:

- Enhance empathy by allowing individuals to experience life through another's perspective.

- Aid in healing by identifying sensory or energetic imbalances in others.
- Expand awareness by enabling the exploration of sensory realities across time and space.

Such mastery requires dedication to understanding the energetic frequencies that govern sensory electricities. By cultivating sensitivity, focus, and resonance, the boundaries of perception can be transcended, unlocking the infinite potential of human consciousness.

Integrating the Story and the Science

The story of the man who could see through the eyes of others serves as a powerful example of the latent abilities within us all. His experience reminds us that the five electricities are not confined to the individual but are part of a universal energetic field that connects all beings. Through focus, intention, and an expanded auric presence, we can begin to tap into these currents, accessing sensory experiences beyond our own.

This phenomenon also aligns with scientific theories such as bioelectric fields and quantum entanglement, suggesting that sensory electricities might operate as interconnected networks. By bridging the metaphysical with the scientific, we gain a deeper understanding of the vast capabilities of the human spirit and the profound unity of all existence.

The Interplay Between the Active and Passive Mind

The relationship between the **active mind** and the **passive mind** is a dynamic interaction that defines the nature of our existence, our manifestations, and our perceptions. Together, they create a symphony of thought, energy, and action, shaping reality itself.

The Role of the Active Mind

The **active mind** serves as the architect of thought, willpower, and creative energy. It projects intention with precision and determines the blueprint for all mental and physical constructions. This projection originates from the higher self, the true "I," which is formless and expansive. The active mind's key characteristics include:

- **Projection of Will**: It exerts force upon the passive mind, planting the "seed" of thought or intention.
- **Creation of Reality**: By directing energy and forming specific thought patterns, it initiates manifestation.
- **Conscious Authority**: It is the aspect of the self that consciously interacts with and directs the passive mind, ensuring alignment with purpose.

When the active mind becomes dormant or weak, external influences can dominate, leading to a life shaped by others' wills rather than one's own intentions.

The Role of the Passive Mind

The **passive mind** acts as the fertile ground, the receptive space where seeds of thought take root and grow. It holds the potential to nurture the intentions planted by the active mind. Its key characteristics include:

- **Receptivity**: The passive mind absorbs and processes the energy and thoughts projected onto it.
- **Formation of Thought**: It organizes and manifests the active mind's input into tangible or mental reality.
- **Susceptibility to Influence**: Without guidance from the active mind, it becomes vulnerable to external forces, assimilating external impressions as its own.

The passive mind becomes the "builder" of the active mind's architectural vision, reflecting either the individual's will or the dominance of stronger external minds.

The Duality of Energy: Masculine and Feminine Forces

At the heart of this interplay lies the **duality of energy**, symbolized by the masculine and feminine principles:

- **Masculine Energy (Magnetic)**: Represents the active force, drawing energy towards itself with intention and focus.
- **Feminine Energy (Electric)**: Represents receptivity, responding to the magnetic force and embodying creativity and nurturing potential.

When these energies unite, they form **electromagnetism**, the essence of vibration and creation itself. The **Source (God)** embodies ultimate magnetism, while creation is the electric field—a reflection of the Creator's will. This dynamic interplay between masculine and feminine energies sustains the act of creation.

The Danger of Passivity Without Awareness

When the passive mind operates without the direction of the active mind, it:

1. **Becomes a Vessel for External Forces**: External minds with stronger willpower or societal influences can project their intentions into the passive mind, shaping one's thoughts and beliefs.
2. **Lives as a Reflection**: Individuals become mere echoes of their environment, losing their authentic self and creative potential.
3. **Falls into Egoistic Entrapment**: Without awareness of the higher self, one becomes confined to the "me" consciousness, entangled in transient emotions and external validation.

This state of passivity breeds ignorance, emotional instability, and a disconnection from the divine.

Awakening Through Active Consciousness

The path to mastery lies in activating the higher mind and aligning it with the passive mind to create harmony and intention. This alignment is achieved through:

- **Meditation**: Quieting the influx of thoughts to access higher consciousness and align with divine will.
- **Conscious Detachment**: Observing emotions and transient experiences without attachment, recognizing them as phenomena passing through the self.
- **Directed Willpower**: Focusing energy with love and clarity toward desired manifestations, ensuring alignment with universal good.

When the active mind projects its will with clarity, and the passive mind receives and nurtures that energy, a powerful cycle of creation is set into motion.

The Magnetic Force of Love and Personal Magnetism

Love, as the ultimate magnetic force, binds all aspects of creation together. It is through love that the active mind influences the passive mind, and through which energy flows effortlessly toward manifestation.

- **Personal Magnetism**: Individuals who exude love and intention project powerful images into the mental spaces of others, leaving lasting impressions. This magnetic force can shape

relationships, influence decisions, and attract opportunities.
- **Avoiding Manipulation**: Awareness of this principle is essential to avoid being unconsciously influenced by external projections, such as advertisements or societal norms.

Mastery Over Emotions and the Mind

By cultivating awareness of the interplay between the active and passive mind, individuals can:

1. **Achieve Emotional Mastery**: Recognize emotions as temporary phenomena, separating them from the eternal higher self.
2. **Awaken True Self-Awareness**: Realize the nature of the "I" as the formless, infinite essence of divine will.
3. **Create with Purpose**: Direct the passive mind to manifest thoughts and desires aligned with universal good.

In this awakened state, individuals transcend the ego and become conscious participants in the divine orchestration of creation.

Manifestation Through Divine Alignment

When the will of the active mind aligns with the will of the Creator, manifestation becomes effortless. This process is enhanced by:

- **Infusing Willpower with Love**: Love amplifies the energy of intention, ensuring alignment with divine principles.

- **Maintaining Focus**: The active mind must remain steadfast in its vision, avoiding distraction and distortion.
- **Universal Good**: Intentions rooted in universal benefit unlock higher knowledge and attract divine support.

The Symphony of Active and Passive Minds

The interplay between the active and passive mind mirrors the eternal dance of creation and Creator. The active mind projects, the passive mind nurtures, and together they manifest reality. By mastering this relationship, individuals unlock their creative potential, align with divine will, and step into their role as conscious co-creators within the universe. This balance of action and receptivity is the foundation of all spiritual growth and the key to transcending the illusions of separateness.

It's The Will That Heals

The power to heal lies in the cultivation and refinement of willpower, a force that allows one to focus their awareness and channel their intention toward well-being and restoration. Healing, at its core, is not merely a physical act but a profound energetic alignment facilitated by the directed energy of the will. A master healer embodies this ability, bringing forth transformative energy to nurture and restore others. By focusing deeply on an individual's needs and projecting the intention for their healing, the healer creates a pathway for wholeness and renewal.

Self-healing is an equally vital and sacred journey, one that reveals the immense metaphysical power within. As a metaphysician, you are inherently equipped with extraordinary capabilities that extend far beyond the physical realm. Within the depths of your being resides a boundless reservoir of healing energy, awaiting your conscious activation. To recognize this power is to acknowledge your divine nature, and to trust in it is to embark on the transformative path of self-mastery. Healing is not an external pursuit but a profound internal alignment with the universal currents of life and vitality.

The Master Healer's Will

A master healer wields the energy of willpower with clarity and intention, aligning their thoughts, emotions, and focus toward the well-being of the individual they seek to heal. Healing is achieved through three core principles:

- **Focused Awareness:** Direct attention to the individual's physical, mental, emotional, or spiritual state. Visualize their well-being with unwavering clarity, holding the image of their restored health in the mind's eye.
- **Channeling Energy:** Act as a conduit for divine energy, channeling it through the self and into the recipient. Use breath, visualization, or affirmations to amplify the flow of healing energy.
- **Setting Intention:** Align the intention for healing with universal principles of love, harmony, and balance. Understand that the healer does not "create" the healing but facilitates the recipient's natural capacity for restoration.

The Path of Self-Healing

Self-healing is both a personal responsibility and a sacred art. The journey of self-healing begins with the recognition that you are the vessel through which divine energy flows. Your body and spirit are interconnected conduits of this force, capable of both receiving and transmitting it. By nurturing this divine energy and cultivating an unwavering belief in your innate abilities, you open the door to profound transformation.

Steps to activate self-healing:

1. **Acknowledge Your Inner Power:** Recognize that healing begins within and that you are the vessel through which divine energy flows. Affirm your belief in your ability to heal and transform.
2. **Cultivate Stillness:** Engage in meditation or contemplative practices to quiet the mind and attune to the subtle energies within. Access the still point of consciousness where healing energy can be harnessed and directed.
3. **Activate the Healing Process:** Visualize areas of imbalance within your body, mind, or spirit. Direct your will to restore harmony, envisioning the flow of light or energy into those areas.
4. **Trust the Process:** Release doubt and fear, trusting in the natural intelligence of the body and spirit to realign with health and vitality. Surrender to the divine flow, allowing the healing to occur in its perfect timing and form.

The Role of the Divine in Healing

Healing is not merely a physical process but a spiritual act of aligning with the universal source of life and love. It is a sacred expression of your connection to the divine. Healing requires trust, intention, and the willingness to embrace your role as both healer and healed.

- **Divine Flow:** Healing energy originates from the Source, often referred to as God or the Creator. The healer becomes a vessel, aligning their will with the divine will to facilitate restoration.
- **Harmony with Universal Laws:** True healing occurs when one harmonizes with the natural rhythms and laws of the universe. This harmony restores balance and removes blockages in the flow of energy.
- **Faith and Conviction:** Healing requires unwavering belief in the process and in the ability to access divine energy. Doubt and fear can hinder the flow of healing energy, while faith amplifies it.
-

The Metaphysician's Journey

As a metaphysician, the journey of self-healing and the ability to heal others is a process of self-mastery. This mastery involves understanding energy dynamics, refining the will, and aligning with higher vibrational frequencies. The act of healing, whether directed outward or inward, is a testament to the transformative power of will and the boundless nature of the human spirit.

- **Understanding Energy Dynamics:** Recognize the flow of energy within yourself and others. Develop the ability to sense, direct, and balance this energy.
- **Refining the Will:** Strengthen your willpower through practice and discipline. Use focused thought, visualization, and meditation to amplify the potency of your will.
- **Aligning with Higher Frequencies:** Elevate your consciousness to resonate with higher vibrational energies. By doing so, you attune to the divine and access the infinite reservoir of healing energy.

Healing as a Path of Transcendence

Healing is not merely about restoring health but about transcending limitations and evolving into higher states of being. Through the act of healing, one can:

- **Discover the True Self:** Unveil the divine essence within and embody it in daily life. Recognize yourself as both the healer and the healed.
- **Expand Awareness:** Deepen your understanding of the interconnectedness of all life. Perceive the unity between the individual and the universal Source.
- **Manifest Divine Potential:** Use the energy of willpower to align with divine purpose. Serve as a beacon of love and light, inspiring healing and transformation in others.

Conclusion

Healing is an act of will, love, and alignment with the divine. Whether you are channeling energy outward or nurturing yourself inwardly, you are both the initiator and the conduit, channeling the Creator's energy to restore balance and harmony. Embrace the path of self-healing and self-mastery, for within you lies the power to transform yourself and others. By cultivating this power, you align with your highest purpose and manifest the divine essence within all aspects of your being.

Kundalini Rising: The Awakening of Dormant Energy

The awakening of Kundalini is achieved through a process of profound absorption in pure consciousness, leading to the attainment of supreme awareness. This state is reached through unwavering concentration, directing your focus toward the core of your being, where the radiant light of consciousness resides. Once this light is discovered, your awareness becomes akin to a spark of light—a luminous force that can be consciously inserted into areas of "interest" or darkness through the deliberate power of will.

The soul interfaces with the physical body through a series of energetic centers known as chakras, which act as vehicles for the flow of consciousness. These centers serve as gateways for awareness, enabling the individual to access immense power as their consciousness elevates.

When the chakras are activated, they transform into dynamic vortexes of energy capable of directing and amplifying Kundalini's flow.

The Light of Consciousness: Activating Kundalini

The journey of Kundalini awakening begins with focused and deliberate absorption in pure consciousness. At the core of this journey lies the radiant light of awareness, serving as the catalyst for the awakening process.

- **Unwavering Concentration:** Train the mind to focus intensely on the present moment and the core of your being, aligning physical, mental, and spiritual energies into a unified field of awareness.
- **Infusion of Awareness:** Direct sparks of consciousness toward the root chakra (Muladhara) through visualization and intentional focus. With repetition, this awakens the dormant Kundalini energy.
- **Ignition and Activation:** Focused attention acts as a spark plug, igniting Kundalini energy. Like a coiled serpent unwrapping, the energy begins its ascent through the central channel, the Sushumna Nadi.
- **Gradual Ascent:** As Kundalini rises, it activates each chakra, unlocking the spiritual, emotional, and physical powers associated with each center. The ascent aligns with your stage of spiritual evolution.
-

The **root chakra**, representing the base of existence, becomes the primary focal point for this deliberate insertion of sparks of awareness.

By repeatedly and intentionally infusing this center with heightened attention, Kundalini begins to stir. This activation causes an intensely luminous light to radiate from within. It is at this precise moment that Kundalini begins its ascent, illuminating and energizing each chakra it traverses.

The Role of Chakras in Kundalini Rising

The chakras are not just energy centers; they are gateways for consciousness and spiritual awakening. As Kundalini ascends, it sequentially activates these centers, unlocking latent powers and transforming the individual.

- **Root Chakra (Muladhara):** The foundation of physical existence. Activation brings stability and grounding, preparing the body for higher spiritual experiences.
- **Sacral Chakra (Swadhisthana):** Associated with creativity and emotions. Awakening enhances creative potential and emotional harmony.
- **Solar Plexus Chakra (Manipura):** Governs personal power and transformation. Activation amplifies confidence and willpower.
- **Heart Chakra (Anahata):** Center of love and unity. Awakening develops compassion and deep emotional healing.
- **Throat Chakra (Vishuddha):** Responsible for self-expression. Activation unlocks inspired and truthful communication.
- **Third Eye Chakra (Ajna):** Seat of intuition and spiritual vision. Awakening sharpens inner knowing and perception.

- **Crown Chakra (Sahasrara):** Gateway to divine consciousness. Full Kundalini ascent culminates here, merging individual awareness with universal intelligence.

The Pathway to Illumination

The practice of unwavering concentration brings forth the illuminating light of knowledge. When you achieve full concentration on a specific object, subject, or area of interest, you can consciously direct sparks of this radiant awareness into that field. This act deepens your understanding and connection with the target of your focus, allowing new layers of insight to emerge.

Concentration not only sharpens the mind but also allows for the seamless flow of universal knowledge. It reveals hidden truths, broadens perception, and aligns the mind with divine intelligence, ensuring that the ascent of Kundalini unfolds harmoniously.

The Experience of Kundalini Rising

As Kundalini ascends through the chakras, the experience is often transformative, encompassing physical, emotional, and spiritual shifts:

- **Physical Sensations:** Tingling, warmth, or vibrations along the spine, accompanied by spontaneous movements or kriyas.

- **Emotional Transformation:** Release of suppressed emotions leads to catharsis and healing, often accompanied by heightened states of joy or peace.
- **Spiritual Awakening:** A profound sense of unity with all creation, visions of sacred geometry, and encounters with divine light or sound.

Integrating Kundalini Energy

The process of Kundalini awakening can be overwhelming without proper grounding and integration. Balance is key to aligning this powerful energy with your physical, emotional, and spiritual well-being.

- **Grounding Techniques:** Spend time in nature, walk barefoot, or practice grounding meditations to stabilize the energy.
- **Meditation and Breathwork:** Regular mindfulness and pranayama ensure the balanced flow of energy throughout the body.
- **Healthy Lifestyle:** Nourish the body with wholesome foods, maintain a disciplined routine, and engage in regular spiritual practices to support the transformation.

The awakening of Kundalini is not merely a physical or energetic phenomenon but a spiritual journey that reveals the interconnectedness of all existence. Through deliberate practice and unwavering focus, you uncover the infinite potential within, aligning your consciousness with the boundless light of creation. This is the true essence of Kundalini rising—an ascent into the luminous realms of higher awareness and divine unity.

Applying Will: Mastery of Mind and Manifestation

The transformative power of **willpower** lies in its ability to align thought, emotion, and action with higher principles and desired outcomes. When the **light of consciousness** and focused intent harmonize, they forge a potent force capable of transcending obstacles, influencing reality, and creating profound personal evolution.

The Veils of Perception

Through **meditative practices** that focus on the waves of consciousness extending beyond one's energetic field, the veils obscuring the **light of the true self** are gradually lifted. This allows for:

- **Direct Perception of Reality**: Free from distortions caused by misunderstandings or misconceptions.
- **Holographic Thinking**: When the mind's eye operates in harmony, thoughts are no longer fragmented. Instead, they take on a holographic, multidimensional quality, offering insights aligned with reality's authentic nature.

In the absence of clarity, misconceptions arise, distorting the essence of reality. True understanding restores balance and alignment, enabling accurate perception and action.

The Duality of Willpower

Negative Willpower

- **Adverse Effects**: Projecting negative energy affects both the sender and the surrounding environment.
- **Susceptible Receptors**: Those unprotected against negativity may absorb and amplify these effects, creating cycles of discord.

Positive Willpower

- **Neutralizing Negativity**: A positive mindset aligns with higher vibrations, rendering negative influences ineffective.
- **The Bulletproof Mind**: A fortified mind becomes impervious to external disturbances, maintaining resilience through unwavering focus on positive outcomes.

Manipulation and Emotional Sovereignty

The Role of Emotions

- Emotions significantly influence **vibrational frequency** and energy signatures.
- External triggers, such as images, sounds, or electromagnetic emissions, are often designed to elicit emotional responses, disrupting vibrational harmony.

Building Emotional Resilience

- Recognize manipulative influences and **fortify emotional strength**.
- By cultivating inner balance, individuals regain control over their energy field, ensuring **sovereignty** over their emotional states.

The Synergy of Willpower and Consciousness

When **willpower** aligns with the **light of consciousness** and is guided by **intuition**, it unlocks extraordinary potential:

1. **Focused Determination:**
   - Concentrated willpower directs energy toward a specific goal.
   - The clarity of intent amplifies the effectiveness of actions.
2. **Illuminated Guidance:**
   - Intuition offers subtle insights that complement conscious effort.
   - Acting upon these insights enhances decision-making and purpose-driven action.
3. **Manifestation and Transformation:**
   - The combination of **willpower** and **conscious awareness** bridges the gap between thought and reality.

    ◦ This synergy enables the manifestation of desired outcomes and promotes personal and universal transformation.

Practical Application of Willpower

1. Redirecting Undesirable States

- When faced with an undesirable mental state:
    1. Identify its **opposite polarity**.
    2. Focus intently on this contrasting aspect until it becomes the dominant state.
    3. Allow your mind to align with the desired condition.

2. Dominance of the Self

- The **self** holds dominion over the mind, which serves as a tool for navigating reality.
- Intense emotional experiences, for example, are not encountered by the self directly but are processed through the mind. This perspective cultivates detachment and mastery over reactive tendencies.

3. The Steps to Mastery

- **Concentration**: Direct attention unwaveringly toward a single object or idea.
- **Contemplation**: Deeply analyze and reflect upon this focus to gain insight.
- **Meditation**: Cultivate stillness to align with universal energies.
- **Manifestation**: Apply learned principles to bring desires into reality.

The Polarization Technique

Harness the power of **polarization** by shifting focus deliberately toward desired states:

1. **Recognize the Current State**:
   - Identify the mental or emotional condition you wish to change.
2. **Visualize the Opposite**:
   - Create a vivid mental image of the desired state, including its associated feelings and outcomes.
3. **Immerse Yourself**:
   - Concentrate deeply on this image until it overrides the undesired state.
4. **Reinforce with Willpower**:
   - Apply unwavering determination to maintain alignment with the desired state.

The Will as the Ultimate Instrument

The **will** is the mechanism through which transformation occurs, a bridge between the self and external reality:

- **Mental Sovereignty**: A strong will governs thoughts, ensuring alignment with the higher self.
- **Healing and Manifestation**: The directed application of willpower restores balance and enables the realization of intentions.

- **Divine Alignment**: When willpower resonates with universal principles, it becomes a conduit for divine wisdom and creation.

By mastering the art of willpower, individuals unlock their innate capacity to shape their reality, achieving harmony, resilience, and fulfillment. Through this process, they not only transform their personal lives but also contribute positively to the greater fabric of existence.

Doer vs. Beggar: Embracing the Active Path

The path illuminated by the divine does not seek blind adoration or passive worship; it calls us to rise above stagnation and engage actively in the transformative process of creation. Within this framework lies the distinction between the beggar and the doer—two states of existence that embody vastly different purposes and energies. The beggar represents a passive, dependent state, relinquishing personal power and relying on external forces for fulfillment. This state perpetuates a cycle of lack, hindering the divine energy from flowing freely. The beggar mindset confines an individual to a life of waiting, hoping for miracles without action, stalling the transformative potential that resides within.

In contrast, the doer embraces the active role of a co-creator in the divine plan. The doer is a vessel of intention and action, allowing the divine will to manifest through their efforts. By embodying this role, we awaken our innate talents and align our aspirations with the higher purpose of creation.

This alignment with divine principles empowers us to act with clarity and purpose, channeling transformative energy into the world. The doer's journey is one of self-realization and engagement, a dance with the divine that brings wisdom, grace, and fulfillment into tangible existence.

The divine call to action is an invitation to recognize and embody our role as co-creators. It challenges us to move beyond passivity and embrace the limitless potential that resides within. Through conscious action, we open the door for divine energy to flow, guiding us toward our highest purpose. By choosing to act in harmony with divine laws, we not only fulfill our personal potential but also contribute to the greater unfolding of universal creation. This process is not merely a duty but an opportunity to express the highest aspects of our being.

The human experience itself is a sacred opportunity for spiritual evolution. As beings endowed with intellect, emotion, and physicality, we are uniquely equipped to navigate the complexities of existence and make conscious choices. This capacity for self-awareness and reflection opens pathways to profound growth, allowing us to transcend limitations and align with divine principles. Life's challenges and interactions become the soil in which virtues like compassion, wisdom, love, and forgiveness are cultivated. Through these virtues, we elevate our consciousness, drawing closer to the divine essence that pervades all things.

To become god-like is not to claim omnipotence but to embody divine qualities in thought, word, and deed. It is the realization of our inherent divinity, expressed through love, harmony, and interconnectedness. This alignment with universal principles is a sacred journey of self-discovery and transformation, wherein we recognize our divine nature and actively manifest it in the world. As humans, we are gifted with the ability to grow into this state of being, contributing to the ongoing evolution of consciousness and creation.

The power of thought is a profound tool in this journey, serving as the foundation of creation itself. The mind, when focused and disciplined, becomes an instrument of immense power. Negative and positive thoughts cannot coexist; the presence of one diminishes the other. This highlights the necessity of mastering the mind, for an untamed mind is susceptible to manipulation by external forces. Similarly, emotional regulation is crucial to maintain sovereignty over one's being. By mastering both mind and emotions, we reclaim our divine authority and align ourselves with the higher currents of universal creation. This mastery is the key to transcending the limitations of the beggar and embracing the transformative power of the doer.

The Dichotomy Between the Active and Passive Mind

The mind operates within a dual framework: **active engagement** and **passive receptivity**. This dynamic interplay shapes our ability to harness intuition, manifest desires, and navigate the complexities of existence.

The Role of the Active Mind

The **active mind** is characterized by:

- **Decisive Action**: It processes, analyzes, and directs focus to specific goals or ideas.
- **Willpower**: It exerts energy to shape reality, influence outcomes, and manifest intentions.
- **Alignment with Intuition**: By remaining attuned to inner wisdom, the active mind embraces the guidance of intuition and transforms it into deliberate action.

An active mind thrives when:

1. **It listens to intuition**: Intuitive insights often arise as fleeting whispers, subtle nudges pointing toward the best course of action.
2. **It acts decisively**: It doesn't hesitate or falter in implementing the knowledge received from within.
3. **It remains self-directed**: Rather than being influenced by external noise, the active mind stays firmly aligned with inner clarity.

The Nature of the Passive Mind

The **passive mind**, in contrast, represents:

- **Receptivity**: It is open to external influences, thoughts, and energies, but often without discernment.
- **Inertia**: Lacking its own momentum, it drifts aimlessly, becoming susceptible to external manipulation.
- **Missed Opportunities**: When intuition speaks, the passive mind hesitates, resulting in inaction and eventual regret.

A passive mind struggles when:

1. **It ignores intuition**: It dismisses the subtle messages of wisdom that arise from within.
2. **It succumbs to external control**: Instead of discerning between authentic guidance and external influences, it absorbs impressions indiscriminately.
3. **It becomes paralyzed by doubt**: Overthinking and hesitation render it unable to act, creating cycles of stagnation.

The Consequences of Ignoring Intuition

Failing to heed the whispers of intuition often leads to:

1. **Missed Opportunities**: Doors that could have opened remain closed, and potential growth is stunted.
2. **Emotional Turmoil**: The regret and "what ifs" weigh heavily on the psyche.

3. **Self-Imposed Hardship**: By neglecting inner guidance, one inadvertently invites challenges that could have been avoided.

This dynamic serves as a **reminder of the power of alignment**—an urgent call to cultivate a balance between receptive listening and decisive action.

Harmonizing the Active and Passive Mind

To bridge the gap between these two states, consider the following practices:

1. **Cultivate Intuition**: Dedicate time to stillness and meditation, creating space for intuitive insights to surface.
2. **Act with Confidence**: When intuition arises, trust its validity and take immediate action to integrate its guidance.
3. **Refine Awareness**: Develop discernment to distinguish between authentic intuition and external noise.
4. **Balance Receptivity and Action**: Embrace moments of quiet reflection while remaining ready to act decisively when clarity emerges.

The Integration of Mind and Intuition

When the **active and passive minds** harmonize, they form a powerful partnership:

- **The passive mind listens**: Receptive to the wisdom of intuition, it remains open and observant.

- **The active mind acts**: Empowered by discernment and willpower, it brings intuitive insights into tangible reality.

Through this integration, the **inner self** becomes the guiding force, creating a life marked by alignment, fulfillment, and fewer regrets. This balanced interplay ensures that we walk the path of least resistance, illuminated by the light of our inner knowing.

Growth and Friends: The Power of Vibrational Alignment

Groups of people resonating on similar vibrational frequencies often form communities with shared purposes or identities. These communities offer a sense of belonging, support, and mutual understanding, serving as fertile ground for personal growth and development. The quality of your environment, including the people and things you allow into it, is a direct reflection of your vibrational state. As the adage goes, the five closest individuals in your life mirror who you are.

As we evolve and expand our consciousness, our alignment with higher frequencies and vibrations often results in a shift in our relationships. Those who no longer share our frequency may drift away naturally, no longer resonating with our new state of being. While this can be challenging—letting go of relationships that were once integral to our lives—it is a necessary part of spiritual growth. It is essential to honor everyone's unique journey and understand that not all paths are meant to align forever.

The Challenges of Shifting Relationships

Spiritual growth often brings changes in how we connect with others. As our vibration rises, some relationships may strain or dissolve altogether. This occurs when the vibrational frequencies of two individuals become incompatible. For example, one person may open themselves to higher frequencies while the other remains at a lower vibrational state, creating a natural divergence.

In some instances, both parties may project negative energy onto each other, amplifying discord. In other cases, the drifting apart occurs without conflict, as their paths evolve in different directions. Trust the process, for every ending paves the way for new connections that align more closely with your current frequency and spiritual path. The ebb and flow of relationships is part of life's natural rhythm, guiding you toward people and experiences that resonate with your growth.

Attracting Connections Aligned with Your Higher Self

As you elevate your consciousness, you begin to attract relationships and experiences that align with your new frequency. These connections are often more supportive, fulfilling, and aligned with your divine purpose. It is important to approach these new relationships with openness and a willingness to grow without clinging or imposing old patterns of attachment.

The process of shedding old relationships and welcoming new ones reflects the universal law of attraction: like attracts like. As your vibration rises, you naturally draw in people and experiences that mirror your newfound frequency. This is one of the most rewarding aspects of spiritual evolution, as it cultivates a deeper awareness of the divine interconnectedness of all things.

Avoiding Vibrational Stagnation

Interestingly, some individuals prefer to surround themselves with those they perceive as less evolved or intelligent. This choice may stem from a desire to maintain a sense of superiority or avoid the discomfort of being challenged by those of equal or greater vibrational alignment. This phenomenon can be likened to "being with the fools instead of the half-wise."

While it may feel easier to stay in such environments, doing so hinders your growth. Awareness of your vibrational frequency and the energy of those around you is crucial. Surround yourself with individuals who uplift and inspire you on your journey, promoting a space of mutual growth and support.

Navigating Vibrational Differences

Highly vibrational individuals often find it challenging to connect with those operating on lower frequencies. This difficulty arises because differing vibrational levels can create tension in relationships. When two people with contrasting frequencies interact, one may need to become more receptive to the other's energy, which can be an uncomfortable adjustment. Alternatively, both may project their energy fields, resulting in a clash that manifests as repulsive disharmony.

However, this is not always the case. In many instances, highly vibrational individuals can uplift those around them, even those at or beyond their own vibrational level. This ability to inspire and elevate others depends on the dynamics of the relationship and the openness of both parties.

The Harmonizing Power of Love

Ultimately, the goal is to achieve harmony with all things, regardless of vibrational differences. This harmony is rooted in the activation of love within—love being the universal force that bridges all divides and unifies all frequencies. When love is the guiding force, relationships become tools for mutual elevation, promoting spiritual growth and the realization of divine unity.

Through love, we learn to navigate differences, uplift others, and remain anchored in the truth of our divine essence. This alignment with love transforms every relationship into an opportunity for growth, connection, and the expansion of consciousness.

Energy exchange through sex

Sexual intimacy is far more than a physical connection; it is an intricate interplay of spiritual, emotional, and energetic exchanges. Each act of intimacy creates an indelible connection, intertwining the energy fields of those involved in ways that can profoundly influence their emotional, mental, and spiritual states. This process transcends the confines of the physical body and penetrates the subtle realms of consciousness, making it an act of great significance and potential impact.

When shared between spiritually inclined partners, intimacy becomes a sacred experience that inspires mutual growth and self-discovery. A spiritually aware partner acts as a mirror, reflecting the other's inner divinity and awakening dormant qualities within. This is similar to how a teacher guides a student towards their inherent potential or how the presence of someone embodying greatness can ignite inspiration. Such connections have the power to elevate both individuals, creating a dynamic interplay where each partner's energy uplifts the other, creating a deeper sense of purpose and spiritual alignment.

Conversely, engaging intimately with individuals who carry unresolved traumas, negative traits, or low vibrational energy can leave a lasting impact on one's energetic field. Negative energy, when exchanged during intimacy, can create imbalances, introducing discordant patterns of thought or behavior. This energetic entanglement may persist, influencing emotional states and spiritual progress long after the physical encounter has ended. It is crucial to recognize that during acts of love, one's energy becomes imprinted upon their partner and vice versa.

These imprints can either serve as catalysts for spiritual elevation or anchors that inhibit growth, depending on the quality of the energy exchanged.

To navigate the profound impact of energetic exchanges, one must approach intimacy with conscious awareness. Choosing a partner who aligns with your values, intentions, and spiritual aspirations ensures that the shared energy creates harmony and mutual upliftment. The power of intimacy lies in its ability to either nurture spiritual evolution or entangle one in the lower vibrational states of another. This underscores the importance of discernment and mindful engagement, transforming sexual connection into a sacred act that honors the divine essence within both individuals.

Intimacy also serves as an opportunity to channel the immense creative power inherent in sexual energy. When approached as a spiritual practice, this energy can be consciously directed to fuel personal growth, creativity, and healing. The concept of sacred sexuality emphasizes the union of mind, body, and soul, elevating the act beyond mere physicality. In this context, sexual energy becomes a transformative force that deepens intimacy and strengthens the spiritual bond between partners, aligning their shared experience with the divine.

The energetic exchange during intimacy is a profound and delicate dance that reflects the vibrational state of those involved. By cultivating self-awareness, setting clear intentions, and aligning with partners who share similar spiritual goals, individuals can elevate their relationships and use the act of love as a tool for mutual enlightenment and growth.

This conscious approach ensures that intimacy remains a sacred and empowering experience, capable of unlocking deeper levels of awareness and connection.

The Influencer

The pursuit of knowledge is a sacred journey that encompasses the entirety of existence. It invites us to explore the divine essence of God, unravel the profound intricacies of the universe, and delve into the mysteries of human nature. Along this path, those who vibrate at a higher frequency hold a unique role, serving as models of elevated thought and energy. These highly vibrational individuals emit waves of energy that influence and uplift the frequencies of others, transforming the energetic landscape simply through their presence. By merely vibrating in the world, their existence contributes to the greater good, embodying the profound truth that the "act of being" can itself be an act of service.

The manifestation process reflects the very essence of creation, much like the formation of atoms. At its core lies the interaction between primordial creative elements and pure energy. Pure energy, akin to the active mind or thought, acts as the driving force and influencer, while the primordial elements symbolize the raw materials of creation, shaping thoughts into concrete realities. These creative elements are inherently drawn to the energy of thought, merging with it to birth tangible manifestations. This dynamic mirrors the transformative power of human intention and underscores the profound truth that our thoughts hold the potential to become reality.

This principle extends to human interactions, where influential individuals act as the nucleus of energetic and organizational systems. These active energy sources project their influence outward, attracting and shaping the minds of those who gravitate toward them. Through their ability to materialize mental constructs into actionable frameworks, influencers create communities, movements, and organizations that reflect their vision and will. The passive minds in these systems align with the influencer's energy, contributing to the realization of shared goals and ideals. This highlights the power of influence as a mechanism for manifestation and creation.

However, this power carries a duality that necessitates caution. Passive minds, when left unguarded, are susceptible to manipulation by external forces, whether from governmental entities, cultural narratives, or unseen energies. Such influences can distort an individual's thoughts, leading to manifestations that stray from divine alignment.To remain in harmony with the Creator's will, one must consciously cultivate a receptive yet discerning mind—receptive not to the influences of other active minds, but to the divine forces and energies that emanate from the Creator. This sacred receptivity is guided by discernment, ensuring that external impressions align solely with divine order and higher truths, rather than the agendas of the world or other fragmented wills.

The essence of willpower can be understood as a projection of a luminous "light code," a thought form infused with clarity, focus, and intention. This light code acts as a blueprint for creation, interacting with the fundamental elements of the universe to shape reality. It establishes a rhythmic momentum, setting into motion the forces necessary to bring a vision to life. By aligning one's willpower with the universal field, the light code invokes synchronicities and opportunities that harmonize with the individual's intentions, facilitating the co-creation of their reality.

The power of the light code is activated through practices that unify thought, emotion, and action. Visualization, affirmations, and conscious intention amplify the strength of willpower, creating a resonance with universal energies. This resonance engages the creative forces of existence, shaping the building blocks of reality to align with one's vision. As individuals cultivate their willpower, they unlock the transformative potential within, channeling the energy of creation to manifest their highest aspirations. Through this sacred process, life becomes a conscious dance of creation, purpose, and divine fulfillment.

Call to Action: Be the Influencer

As we conclude this journey of profound exploration, let us turn to the ultimate invitation—the call to be an **influencer** of divine energy in your world. Everything we have explored, from the **active mind** to the **projection of light codes**, culminates in this truth: you are the portal through which divine energy flows. You are the gateway through which the Creator's will manifests. The power to transform your life, your environment, and your world rests within you.

The act of influence is not limited to external power or control; it is a profound inner state of alignment with the Source. When you center yourself in the divine, your presence alone radiates energy that reshapes the vibrations around you. To be an influencer means to become a living embodiment of divine intention, a beacon of light through which possibilities are created, destinies are shaped, and lives are transformed.

The Metaphysical Significance of Influence

To influence is to act as a nucleus of energy, where the currents of creation converge and emanate outward. Just as atoms are structured by the forces of intention and energy, so too is your life shaped by the focus and clarity of your thoughts. Through your connection to the Source, you hold the capacity to mold raw potential into reality. Your thoughts, when aligned with divine truth, become the primordial creative elements that structure the world around you. This is the essence of true power—not domination, but creation.

When you become the influencer in your life and surroundings, you rise beyond being a mere participant in the world. You become an architect of destiny, a creator of realities. This is the ultimate purpose of the active mind: to project divine intention and energy into the fabric of existence, transforming it into a reflection of higher truth and harmony.

The Responsibility of Influence

With this power comes profound responsibility. Your influence is not a tool for manipulation but a sacred act of co-creation with the Creator. By aligning with the Source, your influence harmonizes with divine order, bringing balance and fulfillment to all it touches. As an influencer, you are called to guard your mind, ensuring that your thoughts and actions are rooted in love, truth, and divine purpose. This discernment protects you from the distortion of fragmented wills and aligns you with the higher energies that elevate and expand.

To be an influencer is to live consciously. It is to recognize that your energy, your intentions, and your very being ripple across the universe, creating waves of transformation. By cultivating your willpower, refining your mental focus, and embracing your role as a channel for divine energy, you step into the fullness of your potential.

The Call to Create

Now is the time to take action. Let the knowledge within this book ignite your purpose. Let the truths explored here awaken the infinite possibilities within you. Begin by centering yourself in Source, allowing the light of divine energy to flow through you unimpeded. With every thought, every intention, and every action, be the influencer who brings divine love and harmony into the world. Create fearlessly. Act purposefully. Influence with integrity.

Your life is your canvas. Your mind is your brush. Your connection to the Creator is your palette of infinite colors. Go forth and paint the masterpiece of your existence. Shape your reality with wisdom, love, and unwavering clarity. Let your influence radiate so powerfully that it inspires others to awaken their own potential and align with the Source.

You are the light. You are the gateway. You are the influencer. Step boldly into this role, and together, let us create a world that reflects the boundless energy and love of the Creator. The power is within you—activate it, embody it, and transform all that you touch.

~Ancient

Appendix: Subtitles by Topic

- **Aim: Entering Pure Consciousness** – Pg. 126
- **Aligning with Purpose** – Pg. 60
- **An Advanced Technique for Deepening Concentration** – Pg. 117
- **Awakening through Active Consciousness** – Pg. 170
- **Belief Shapes Reality** – Pg. 143
- **Begin with the Body** – Pg. 41
- **Breaking the Cycle** – Pg. 51
- **Breaking the Cycle of Karma** – Pg. 56
- **Clothes and Energy** – Pg. 22
- **Coming to Terms** – Pg. 34
- **Concentration versus Artificial Intelligence** – Pg. 114
- **Creating a Healthy Space** – Pg. 75
- **Designing with Nature, Materials, and Shapes** – Pg. 73
- **Demonstrating Your Potential** – Pg. 83
- **Dissolving into Universal Consciousness** – Pg. 128
- **Doer vs. Beggar** – Pg. 187
- **Do's and Don'ts** – Pg. 40
- **Energy Exchange through Sex** – Pg. 197
- **Energetic Tools and Enhancements** – Pg. 74
- **Epigenetic Feelings** – Pg. 92
- **External Ecosystem** – Pg. 72
- **Fear** – Pg. 137
- **Harnessing Zeal and Mental Focus** – Pg. 125

- Harmonizing the Active and Passive Mind – Pg. 192
- Imagery Technique: Becoming the Master Architect – Pg. 130
- Inanimate Objects – Pg. 32
- Internal Ecosystem – Pg. 68
- Intuitive Positioning – Pg. 14
- It's the Will That Heals – Pg. 172
- Karma – Pg. 53
- Karma and the Law of Cause and Effect – Pg. 55
- Kundalini Rising – Pg. 177
- Living in Illusion – Pg. 99
- Living the Wisdom – Pg. 80
- Living with Words of Power – Pg. 61
- Mastering the Mind – Pg. 65
- Mastery over Emotions and the Mind – Pg. 171
- Mental Hygiene – Pg. 36
- Manipulation and Emotional Sovereignty – Pg. 183
- Mind Control – Pg. 30
- Neutralizing and Breaking Spells – Pg. 52
- Poverty as an Illusion – Pg. 143
- Positive Affirmation – Pg. 62
- Prayer: The Art of Creative Visualization – Pg. 133
- Practical Application of Willpower – Pg. 185
- Psychic and Spiritual Abilities – Pg. 152
- Psychic Energy – Pg. 16
- Repairing the Auric Field – Pg. 20
- Responsible Attitude – Pg. 24

- **Sexual Imagery** – Pg. 37
- **Sound** – Pg. 28
- **Spirituality versus Religion** – Pg. 65
- **Spiritualized Atom** – Pg. 153
- **Take Action** – Pg. 77
- **Taming the Mind through Imagination** – Pg. 132
- **Technique for Trauma** – Pg. 43
- **The Art of Observation and Concentration** – Pg. 116
- **The Art of Self-Generated States** – Pg. 97
- **The Case for a Fruit-Centered Diet** – Pg. 70
- **The Connection between Heart and Throat Chakra** – Pg. 59
- **The Courage to Act** – Pg. 80
- **The Dichotomy between the Active and Passive Mind** – Pg. 190
- **The Fiddle** – Pg. 45
- **The Five Electricities** – Pg. 155
- **The Geometric Symphony of Creation** – Pg. 129
- **The Inner Light Revealed** – Pg. 128
- **The Interplay between the Active and Passive Mind** – Pg. 167
- **The Journey Back to Harmony** – Pg. 71
- **The Journey of Self-Realization** – Pg. 67
- **The Law of Compensation and Purpose** – Pg. 50
- **The Limits of Human perception** - Pg. 106
- **The Magnetic Force of Love** – Pg. 145
- **The Master Teacher's Role** – Pg. 79
- **The Nature of the Passive Mind** – Pg. 191
- **The Nameless** – Pg. 151

- The Path to Liberation – Pg. 53
- The Path to Mastery – Pg. 42
- The Planetary Impact of Words – Pg. 58
- The Polarization Technique – Pg. 186
- The Power of Divine Alignment – Pg. 126
- The Power of Positive Speech – Pg. 60
- The Power of Thought – Pg. 54
- The Process of Action – Pg. 78
- The Role of Air, Water, and Nature – Pg. 74
- The Role of LOVE and the Master Teacher – Pg. 77
- The Role of Self-Image in Physical and Mental Health – Pg. 123
- The Source as Truth and Knowledge – Pg. 64
- The Spiritual Dimensions of Food – Pg. 70
- The Spiritualized Atom – Pg. 153
- The Synergy of Willpower and Concentration – Pg. 184
- The Transformation of Thought into Reality - Pg. 108
- The Use of Altars – Pg. 119
- The Vibrational Impact of Food – Pg. 69
- Thought Form – Pg. 8
- Time: The Key to Causality – Pg. 102
- Transcend Bodily Impulses – Pg. 42
- Watch Your Tone – Pg. 26
- Words, Knowledge, and Faith – Pg. 60
- Words of Power – Pg. 57
- You Are the Drug – Pg. 96
- You Can't Lead If You Can't See – Pg. 81

www.ingramcontent.com/pod-product-compliance
Lightning Source LLC
Chambersburg PA
CBHW061444300426
44114CB00014B/1834